T0196061

Find Purpose in Your Life
A New Day Dawning

Inspiration   Hope   Confidence   Adventure   Accomplishment

ROBERT SAUNDERS

WESTBOW
PRESS®
A DIVISION OF THOMAS NELSON
& ZONDERVAN

WestBow Press books may be ordered through booksellers or by contacting:

WestBow Press
A Division of Thomas Nelson & Zondervan
1663 Liberty Drive
Bloomington, IN 47403
www.westbowpress.com
1 (866) 928-1240

ISBN: 978-1-9736-0498-3 (sc)
ISBN: 978-1-9736-0499-0 (e)

Library of Congress Control Number: 2017914728

Print information available on the last page.

WestBow Press rev. date: 9/28/2017

Contents

Preface

We all have a purpose in this life that we are uniquely designed to fulfill. However, life is full of obstacles, distractions, and endless patterns that can make this objective hard to discover. This book has been written to help you find your unique purpose sooner rather than later.

This is a guidebook to lead you through an interactive journey to find your purpose in this world. You will explore what has influenced who you are today and define the key components of your individual uniqueness. You will build on this foundation to discover a special purpose for your life, and become able to enjoy personal fulfillment beyond anything you have imagined.

As you embark on this journey, you need to recognize that it may not always follow a simple path. You may experience changes—even surprises—that cannot be anticipated. You may learn new skills, grow as an individual, and find a whole new purpose for your life. That's okay! Embrace positive changes!

As you have gravitated to this book to find answers, I have been chosen, inspired, and guided to produce this book to help you find those answers.

Beginning Pep Talk

You need a dream regarding who you want to become because such a dream can drive you to make it your reality. If you don't have a dream now, don't worry—this book will help you develop one that fits you and motivates you to become all you are meant to be.

To progress toward your dream, you need hope for a better tomorrow. Without hope, there is nothing to strive for. If you are struggling with hope, if you are feeling discouraged, don't be afraid—keep reading! The thoughts and guidance humbly offered in this book will encourage that seed of hope within you to grow. I will guide you through some exercises to help you infuse hope into your life, and you will discover (or rediscover) the greatness you were made to attain—your purpose in life. You are worthy. You are smart. You have great potential. You can achieve your dream and bring incredible value to the world.

In moving forward, your choices are vital to your overall success and fulfillment. Please take the following suggestions seriously.

First, let go of your negativity. Give up finding all the reasons why something can't or won't work. Enter this book with a mind open to "What if?"

Second, let go of your past baggage. While your past can certainly shape you, it is past history, and you can't change it. Your experiences are important, but focus on positive aspects and events, not those that drain your energy. Let go of past failures but keep your learning experiences. Let go of blaming others for hurting you. Don't discount the pain, but remember that you get what you focus on. If you focus on the negative things people have done to you, you cannot move forward. Just let go. Start fresh. It's never too late to start fresh!

Every new day is the first day of the rest of your life!

Third, smile. Some of this material will provoke thought, but our lives shouldn't be approached too seriously. Creating and fulfilling your dream—your purpose—is deep work, but approach it with a sense of humor.

This book will help you develop a meaningful purpose in your life. Along this journey, you will explore your expectations, personality, relationships, experiences, interests, talents, dreams, passions and inner needs to help you understand both who you are today and who you can become. You will also learn about prioritizing and setting goals. While exploring these skills, seek to discover a purpose greater than you have imagined possible.

Make It Personal

Your Life Is Important!

Even if you feel you have achieved great goals already, don't miss this opportunity to discover an even greater destiny!

Understand this is not a book to read and set aside. It is intended to take you through an interactive journey to help you achieve your true purpose. You will reap benefits directly proportional to the thought and effort you put into these activities described below.

- Truly study the material in each section of this book.
- Think about how you can apply this material to your own life.
- Complete the "Stop. Think. Apply." (STA) exercises within each section.

Because this journey is yours, it requires your participation! This book has been organized into topics of manageable length so you can plan your journey to fit your schedule. The questions and exercises at the end of each section are to help you apply the material to yourself. This step will be exciting. It will help you develop and understand your purpose.

Note: If you are reading the e-book version, print out the STA exercises before you read each section, and keep them in a binder where you can complete them and use them for easy reference.

If you skip this interactive part, you won't get the full value of the book. Please pause, ponder, and complete each STA section. Now that you understand how this journey can work best for you, let's start!

1. A Very Familiar Story

Expectations and Reality

Meet Joe—a regular guy who has graduated from school and looks forward to providing the lifestyle he desires for himself and his family. Every person has his or her own story and hopes of fulfilling a unique purpose. You may see yourself in this story because it is about a person who might represent you. So let's begin!

Following graduation, Joe interviewed with various companies, hoping to find a job where he could apply his education and enjoy his work. He found factors he liked at every place he interviewed—yet he also found aspects that didn't suit him. But he concluded that the world was not perfect, and he picked the apparent best option.

Joe was excited when he began his new job. But after a few years, he began to realize that his daily work activities didn't interest him anymore. He wanted to learn new skills and have more responsibilities and challenges. He became resigned to trudging on, day after day, with no enthusiasm. He felt trapped in a place where he didn't want to be, and he kept thinking that there had to be a better way. But he didn't know where to turn for answers.

One day Joe was talking with his friend Bill about his career and its dead end. Bill, who was a couple of years older than Joe, said he understood Joe's feelings because he had gone through the same realization a few years back. He mentioned that a wise mentor named Paul had helped him develop a much more fulfilling life. Paul's process of guiding him took some time and required developing unique insights into himself before he could develop a dream for greater achievement. Because of Paul's guidance, Bill said, he had found a purpose and a level of personal fulfillment that he had never imagined possible. Intrigued, Joe asked Bill how he might contact Paul, and he left with Paul's phone number.

Joe called the next day and set an appointment to meet with Paul. This was new territory for him, and after the phone call, he felt a little apprehensive about the meeting. He was particularly concerned about the process Bill had mentioned to him. He had no idea what he might discover while developing unique insights into his personal identity.

Note to the reader: As you embark on this journey with Joe, you are probably curious about what you might discover within yourself. Have hope that you will learn and grow—and enjoy the journey!

On the day of his appointment, Joe woke up with a feeling of anticipation. He arrived a few minutes early and found Paul waiting for him at the top of the driveway. He was a relatively tall, middle-aged man with a well-groomed, graying beard and a warm smile that helped Joe relax a bit. As they walked toward the office, Joe noticed that Paul seemed to be in excellent physical condition, and his posture was very straight—as if he might have been a marine. Paul showed Joe into his office and asked him to sit on a brown leather sofa. Paul faced him from a large wooden rocker that had obviously been used for many years.

Paul began, "Tell me about yourself, Joe, and why you have come to me."

"When I finished my education and entered the workforce," Joe said, "I had an expectation that I could advance in my job and develop an enjoyable lifestyle. This hasn't happened, and I seem to have lost a sense of purpose in my life."

"I understand, Joe. Most ambitious people tend to get frustrated in today's industrial society. Let me help you see why this is true. While people are all pretty much the same from a biological perspective, we are also distinct—and it is our differences that define our individuality and enable us to make our lives all we want them to be.

"Every business, however, creates work environments to meet its own requirements without consideration for the individuality of its employees. Very simply, they have tasks that need to be performed, and they have defined those tasks so that almost anyone can do them. Therefore, someone with ambition, like you, can become dissatisfied by having personal growth restricted with mundane tasks.

"You, Joe, are a unique and wonderful creation. I want both of us to understand your uniqueness, because these qualities will enable you to become who you are destined to be."

"Is that really possible?"

"Yes, it is. I've helped many people discover their uniqueness and purpose in life—men and women from different cultures and backgrounds, with various skills and economic experiences— and I believe I can help you do the same."

Joe sighed. "I'd like that."

"Good! Then I'd like you to compare the expectations you had when you entered the workforce with the reality you have experienced."

"I expected to have a meaningful job with a real sense of purpose to guide me toward the success I desire. But I'm living in a gap between my expectations and my reality. I feel trapped, and I don't know how to get unstuck. I try to keep myself busy doing things I enjoy in my spare time, but I struggle every day with a lack of purpose. I've thought about getting a different job, but my friends tell me the places they work are no better than where I am now."

"Joe, it's not unusual to experience a difference between your expectations and the reality of living in the world. Sometimes our results are just not what we want them to be, particularly for people with ambition. I'm not surprised by your experience, and I'm glad you were led to me for help.

"For many people, earning a living is a primary focus. And if they don't find significance in their jobs, they float along on the stream of life without specific direction. Commonly, people try to fill the gap with activities or possessions—but without purpose in their lives, this gap will persist. What have you done, Joe?"

"I purchased a boat, and on summer weekends, I take my family camping on the shore of a nearby lake. The problem is that I'm always ready to go back there within a day of getting back home. I get a negative feeling when I go back to work. I can't seem to keep the positive feelings I have when we are at the lake."

"Trying to fill your gap with activities is just a temporary fix, Joe. No activity can completely fill the gap you experience."

"I really enjoy my boat," Joe replied with a sigh, "and I never thought of it as a way to fill the gap in my life. You make me feel even more discouraged. What can I do?"

"Joe, I will lead you on a journey of discovery that will provide some meaningful answers. We'll discover what you are good at and what special gifts you have. We'll talk about how your personality, relationships, and experiences have shaped you and how the cornerstones of your life make you a unique person in this world. We will also explore other priorities in your life because your purpose—and your personal fulfillment—involve much more than just what you do to earn a living. You came to me to find a more fulfilling career, so we will address this topic first. However, we will also discuss other priorities that affect your purpose. This journey will be both exciting and extremely rewarding. It may take time to find the purpose you desire, but you will never regret achieving such a goal."

Joe asked, "Is this part *developing unique insights into myself*? That's how Bill described it."

"Could be, Joe. Are you ready to tackle the first area?"

"Yes! Let's do it."

Stop. Think. Apply.

Consider Your Story: Expectations and Reality

What were your expectations upon entering the working world?

_____

_____

_____

_____

What are the realities you have discovered in this environment?

_____

_____

_____

_____

Do you experience a gap between your expectations and your realities?

_____

_____

_____

_____

How do you feel about having this gap?

_____

_____

_____

_____

What have you done to try to fill the gap?

_____

_____

_____

_____

What else do you believe you can do to fill the gap?

_____

_____

_____

_____

Is this just a temporary fix, or might it represent real progress?

_____

_____

_____

_____

Why do you feel this way?

_____

_____

_____

_____

Have hope! Believe you can close that gap. Your journey is about to begin!

Personal Notes

2. Understanding Who You Are

2.1. Personality

Paul opened their next meeting with the statement, "Joe, you have many facets that make you unique as a person, and the driving force is your personality. Your personality is like your operating system. It is involved in everything you do, and it influences how you think and act at a subconscious level. Identifying your personality is not an exact science, but it can be a revelation to learn how and why you react in certain situations.

"Understanding the strengths and weaknesses of your own personality type, plus the personality types of the people you interact with regularly, can significantly influence your success. Learning to identify other people's personality types can help you understand why they think and act the way they do. Then you can interact with them more effectively. This can be a significant advantage in your interpersonal relationships, whether at work or with family and friends."

Looking surprised, Joe responded, "Personality sounds a lot more involved than I ever realized, and you make it sound important."

"It's very important, Joe. The concept of personality styles goes all the way back to Hippocrates in ancient Greece. Some people have defined a complex matrix of personality styles, but for simplicity's sake, I will just consider four, most common, personality styles. I will gloss over them to give you some understanding of the important differences, but I will give a reference to guide you into deeper study if you want to know more. You may find you don't totally fit a single personality style, as most people are strongly one style with a secondary, less pronounced one as well. Before defining styles, however, let's put some structure to the analysis. Some people are very socially interactive and tend to express themselves well. These people are also viewed as talkative and energetic. We call these people *extroverts* because they are usually very interested in the world around them and in interacting with that world.

"Other people are usually quieter and less outgoing. These people are referred to as *introverts* and are not generally considered the life of the party. They tend to be observers rather than participants. Introverts are more focused on the world inside themselves. They are not necessarily self-centered people, but they observe the world and internalize their thoughts about it. Are you following thus far?"

"Yes," answered Joe. "I see some people who are apparently extroverts or introverts. But there are some I'm not so sure about. What about those people?"

"I'm glad you asked. Extroversion and Introversion are two ends of a personality scale. Most people don't fall at either extreme but fit somewhere along the scale between them. You might also find that, in certain situations, you tend to shift position along this scale. It's normal to have a bit of both traits. What you want to identify is your primary type."

"As you say, sometimes I'm more one way, and other times I might be more the other. So, on a scale from black to white, so to speak, I tend to be a shade of gray a lot of the time."

Nodding, Paul continued, "Understanding which way you tend to be most of the time will help you identify jobs, tasks, dreams—and a purpose—that will be strengthened by your personality. For example, if you are an extreme introvert, working in public sales might be very draining for you. Not that you couldn't do it, but relating to a lot of people might be a constant struggle, especially if you don't have significant time to recharge between interactions.

"Now that you have an introductory grasp on introversion versus extroversion, let's move onto another nuance of your personality. Joe, would you say you are more a people-driven person or a task-driven one?"

Looking puzzled, Joe responded, "You have to help me here. Please explain those terms."

"A people-driven individual likes being around people, whether as an observer or interacting with individuals. It also means you are concerned about people's feelings and don't want to offend them. Task-driven people, however, are less focused on feelings and more focused on information and tasks that need to be done. Certainly they still have feelings, but they perceive their environments differently and tend to come across as less empathetic at times. What is important to them is accomplishing something—completing a significant task."

"So," Joe asked, "Is this concept a sliding scale like being somewhere between an introvert and an extrovert?"

"Yes, it is. Now let me give you a visual picture of how these two scales interact to create four distinct personalities. The animal references are to help you envision the personality type.

	Task-driven	People-driven
Extroverted	lion the driver	chimpanzee the expressive
Introverted	giraffe analytical	turtle amiable

"Let me give you some insight into each of these personality types.

"The driver (a lion), an extroverted, task-driven, power-seeking type with leadership qualities, strives to get tasks done. This person is ambitious, energetic, and forceful. The lion is an effective representative of this personality style. The lion can be aggressive and a leader. The lion is a strong-willed, decisive, and bold operator. Lion types are independent, self-sufficient people, confident that they are right.

"The expressive (a chimpanzee) is an extroverted, people-driven, pleasure-seeking, sociable optimist. The chimpanzee type is collaborative, excitable, and fun. One of the most expressive animals, the chimpanzee is an excellent example of this personality style. They are the life of a party, easily amused. The chimpanzee person is very sociable, enthusiastic, curious, and charismatic. Other people may tend to follow such a person to be part of the excitement.

"The analytical type (a giraffe) is a reader: a task-driven, analytical, detail-oriented, independent, and meticulous person. The giraffe represents this personality because it is aloof. The giraffe personality tends to study what is going on around it instead of being a more active participant. Serious and purposeful, the giraffe becomes an expert and pays close attention to details.

"The amiable (a turtle) is an introverted and people-driven person. Relaxed, peaceful, helpful to others, patient, humble, and amiable, they seek balance and are faithful friends. The turtle is quiet and keeps feelings hidden. Even though the turtle is friendly, at any hint of danger or threat, the turtle will quickly retreat to the safety of its shell. The turtle is a sweet and tender personality. Turtle types tend to stick with the paths they have chosen; they are not going to be easily swayed when making choices unless they are concerned about others' feelings.

"Joe, how do you feel about these concepts? Does this help you understand a little more about yourself—perhaps more about other people too? Do you think that understanding this a little bit might help you be more effective when dealing with others? Perhaps you will begin to see how they are motivated or what helps make them feel more at ease."

"This is a lot of information to absorb, but I think that, with practice, I can learn to relate to other people more effectively. I've always known I have a personality, but I didn't realize there were certain traits that characterize people like this. Paul, are you a giraffe? I can tell that details are important to you, and you don't seem overly outgoing—even though here, one-on-one, you don't seem shy."

"Very observant of you, Joe. I'm very much a giraffe, but I do enjoy working with people, which gives me some turtle characteristics. My comfort in social situations has come with years of practice, so while I might not seem shy, that is how I am naturally."

"What type of animal am I, Paul?"

"I want you to decide what fits you best and listen to your gut. If you feel very strongly about something, you should consider it. Understanding the strengths and weaknesses of your personality style can help you decide whether you want to be an employee or a business owner. For example, if you're a detail-oriented type like a giraffe, you are probably more suited to the administrative or accounting side of a business, while more expressive people take care of finding new customers, closing deals, and supporting those customers."

"I'm beginning to see how understanding my personality might help lead me to a more fulfilling career."

"Joe, you might clearly see yourself as one of these four personality types, or you might see a blend of two of them. Some people are very strongly one type, and others aren't. There is no perfect answer to personality. I just want to give you information and ideas regarding both your personality style and that of other people. By understanding other people's personality styles, you can adjust how you interact with them to have more effective communications.

"Remember, Joe, these are general descriptions and concepts. If you want to learn more, you can search the Internet and try taking a Meyers-Briggs Type Indicator (MBTI) test, [1] which defines sixteen unique personality types and may provide more insight, depending on what your needs are. If this concept is frustrating for you, please take a breath. You need simply to acknowledge that you have a special and unique personality, and you can use that personality to shine in your relationships with other people."

Note to the reader: If you are dissatisfied with a current job, understanding personality types, yours and other people's, may help you become more successful without requiring you to change jobs.

Stop. Think. Apply.

Understanding Who You Are

Personality

Highlights

- Everyone falls somewhere on a scale between introversion and extroversion.
- Similarly, everyone fits on a scale between the task-driven lion and people-driven turtle.
- Most people generally fit into one of the four major personality styles or a blend of a couple of styles.
- Understanding your predominant personality style will help you in all aspects of your life.

Application

In a group setting, are you
outgoing _____ or do you stay to yourself? _____

Do social situations tend to drain you of energy?
Yes _____ No _____

Mark where you believe you are on the following scale.

|_____|_____|_____|_____|_____|_____|_____|

Introvert   **Extrovert**

Now mark where you think you are on this scale.

|_____|_____|_____|_____|_____|_____|_____|

Task-driven   **People-driven**

How do these scales help you understand yourself as a person?

_____

_____

_____

_____

Note: Evaluating your personality should provide perspective and insight to help you evaluate your ideal working environment and your personal relationships. Your personality is always working subconsciously, driving how you interact with others.

What do you think might be your primary personality style?

_____
_____
_____
_____

What makes you think this is true?

_____
_____
_____
_____

If you think you have a secondary personality style, what is it?

_____
_____
_____
_____

How will this information help you in your personal life?

_____
_____
_____
_____

How will this information help you in your work environment?

_____
_____
_____
_____

Note: Your personality is neither good nor bad. It just is. So understanding this aspect of who you are can facilitate better relationships with others in every part of your life.

Would you prefer to work
as part of a team? _____   or independently? _____

What are your thoughts and feelings regarding what you have learned about your personality?

_____

_____

_____

_____

Personal Notes

2.2. Relationships

As Joe settled into Paul's office, Paul explained, "Mankind was not created to live in isolation. We are designed to be social creatures—interfacing with other people for a variety of reasons, including love, support, laughter, guidance, strength, shared work, and many others. While mankind has special attributes, such as the ability to reason, many of our attributes also apply to the entire animal kingdom. It is essential for similar animals to pair up to support each other throughout their lives, and to ensure that their species will continue to exist in the future."

Family

The most significant personal relationships are those with one's immediate family—our parents and, perhaps, brothers and sisters. It is within this group that each generation learns the meaning of being loved, basic needs are fulfilled, and we are guided and trained to live with other people in this world. As the young mature, they may get to know their extended family—grandparents, aunts, uncles, and cousins, plus other more distant relatives. This exposure can greatly enrich our lives, helping us understand where we come from and who we are. It can also contribute to who we become as independent adults. Very simply, we are nurtured and formed within our immediate and extended family.

Our family can also be a wonderful source of support and guidance as we face challenges and learning experiences. Family members can provide encouragement, accountability, and a safe place. In addition, if we have children, they can be a source of great pleasure as we watch them grow and mature into responsible adults.

Every person experiences a variety of relationships beyond the family—each with its own level of familiarity and personal commitment. Let's briefly consider relationships beyond the family and how they can affect your life.

Friends

These people share experiences and create memories with you. Treasure these relationships because a circle of good friends can enrich your life significantly. You can enjoy sharing experiences with these people and learn and grow through these associations. True friends know who you are and respect and trust you deeply. They are the people who will stand with you in good times and bad. Your support network includes people you can count on in the middle of the night during a crisis—and who will laugh with you as you grow older and wiser together.

Note: Negative relationships can be toxic to your personal character, so learn to minimize them to keep your life as positive as possible. Songwriter Johnny Mercer wrote lyrics on this theme in the 1930s.

You've got to accentuate the positive
Eliminate the negative
Latch on to the affirmative
Don't mess with Mister In-Between.
("Accentuate the Positive" by Johnny Mercer)

Romantic

We all need to be loved and appreciated, and favorable attention from someone of the opposite sex can be a powerful attraction. As human beings, we have an emotional element that can be nurtured and supported by such a relationship to produce joy and fulfillment beyond our imagination.

Here's a true story: A man I knew boarded a Fifth Avenue bus in New York years ago and climbed the stairs to the upper level. He looked over the available seats and sat next to a young lady who had attracted his attention. Three blocks later, they got off the bus, got a marriage license, and enjoyed a great marriage for over fifty years. The significance of this story: you never know when you might meet a person with whom you can share a wonderful life.

Professional

These are people we work with on a regular basis. Develop meaningful relationships with the colleagues to whom you relate well, and they can become part of a business (and sometimes personal) network that supports you throughout your entire career.

Mentors

A mentor is a personal guide who understands your strengths and weaknesses and is willing to teach you how to grow, both personally and professionally, to reach your full potential. A mentor can be one of the most powerful influences in your life, so look for someone with experience and wisdom who might be willing to become such a guide for you.

A good mentor will hold you accountable on a regular basis. He/she will hold your feet to the fire as required to help you achieve your desired results according to a mutually-agreed plan.

People in Your Path

Most people are so wrapped up in what they have done or plan to do that other people in near proximity remain anonymous to them. Unfortunately, today's pace of life and the technology we carry with us encourage such focus.

Being open to interactions with other people in the course of your daily life, however, could lead to significant benefits. You never know who you might meet in a casual conversation, and the outcome of such a short connection may ultimately provide a life-changing opportunity.

Stop. Think. Apply.

Understanding Who You Are

Relationships

Highlights

- Relationships are important!
- Your family should be your safe place for encouragement and personal accountability.
- People around you are important because those with whom you associate will influence you.
- A good mentor can guide you and help you achieve your full potential.

Application

Do you have members of your family who can encourage you and support you? Who are they?

_____

_____

_____

_____

Who are your closest friends, and why do you treasure them?

_____

_____

_____

_____

Who might be a potential mentor for you?

_____

_____

_____

_____

Personal Notes

2.3. Experiences

As Joe arrived, Paul opened their discussion. "Joe, your personality and relationships are very important, but don't discount the significance of your experiences and how they have shaped you."

"What do you mean, Paul?"

"Let me explain. Your experiences are very personal and may involve a complex mixture of visions, feelings, thoughts, and reactions to events that have happened to you or around you. They can be a strong force that holds you back from personal growth. Or the knowledge and wisdom you gain from your experiences can help you evaluate events that occur in your future. This background continues to evolve throughout your entire life, influencing how you see yourself, how you react to the world around you, and who you become as a person."

Joe responded, "I never realized how deeply my experiences can affect me. Can events that happened years ago really affect me later in life?"

"They definitely can, Joe—both positively and negatively. While many of your experiences may be good, some might be not so good. You want to learn and grow from your experiences without being limited or controlled by them.

"Every day when you wake up, I want you to have hope that you really can find a great purpose in your life and can make your life all you want it to be—in spite of events that may have happened to you or around you. So please write this down and put a legible copy of it where you can read it each morning:

'Every new day is the first day of the rest of my life!'"

Stop. Think. Apply.

Understanding Who You Are

Experiences

Highlights

- Experiences influence who you are.
- You can't change the past, so learn appropriate lessons from your experiences and move on with your life.
- Have hope! Focus on the positive and make your future what you want it to be.

Application

How have your past experiences influenced you?

_____
_____
_____
_____

What important lessons have you learned from your past experiences?

_____
_____
_____
_____

What types of experiences do you seek?

_____
_____
_____
_____

Have you had experiences you'd like to put behind you?

_____
_____
_____
_____

There is only one way to make this happen—decide to put those experiences behind you! Are you willing to make such a decision today?

Yes _____   No _____

Why do you feel this way?

_____

_____

_____

_____

What will you focus on to make your future what you want it to be?

_____

_____

_____

_____

Personal Notes

3. Recognize Your Individuality

3.1. Interests

Paul opened their next meeting with an introduction. "Joe, I want to introduce you to a few things that will be fundamental to finding a meaningful purpose for your future. Your interests are a good place to start because they are strong indicators of where you can be fulfilled. I'd like to know what interests you have, but before you answer, let me define what I mean. An interest is usually triggered through your senses, and then you investigate it to see how you like it. When you find a topic or activity that attracts your attention, you may invest time and energy to learn more about it. If you pursue something on a continued basis—and it grows into a strong desire—take note! This is the kind of interest that can be important in your life."

Joe responded, "Why do you think my interests are so important?"

"I believe your interests are among the cornerstones that define your uniqueness as a person. Let me ask you, Joe, do you understand what a cornerstone is?"

"Sure—it's what supports a corner of a building."

"Yes, and the kind of cornerstone we are talking about here supports your life. Each of us has important factors that make us uniquely who we are. With this definition in mind, Joe, what are your particular areas of interest?"

"Gee, I like a lot of things."

"Good. As you think back through your life, have there been particular things that repeatedly attracted your attention for a number of years? It might be something you like reading about, or something you have been drawn to and would like to have in your life. For example, a boat was certainly an interest of yours—and you read about them, thought about them, looked at them, and eventually purchased one for yourself. From what you have said, you get a lot of enjoyment out of using it.

"Now I want you to get in touch with other things that interest you. Just like the fulfillment you have with your boat, you probably have other things you think about, read about, and maybe even look at on occasion. You need to get in touch with these other things and make a list of them so you can prioritize what is truly important to you. As you are searching for real purpose in your life, some of these things may develop into cornerstones on which you can begin to build your future."

Stop. Think. Apply.

Recognize Your Individuality

Interests

Highlights

- Everyone has interests—particular things that attract and hold their attention.
- Your interests are part of what make you unique.
- Some interests can grow into strong internal desires—even passions—that can change your life.

Application

Make a list of things you loved as a child.

_____

_____

_____

_____

List pursuits that interest you now (TV, books, activities, news stories, volunteering, sports, or the like).

_____

_____

_____

_____

What types of articles do you read regularly?

_____

_____

_____

_____

Why do these interest you?

_____

_____

_____

_____

What things have been of interest to you for a relatively long time and may have created a strong internal desire? (Note: This type of interest can develop into a passion!)

_____

_____

_____

_____

What is it about these things that you find particularly intriguing or exciting?

_____

_____

_____

_____

How do you participate in your areas of interest? Is it by observation, study, or direct participation?

_____

_____

_____

_____

Have you ever thought about participating in any area of interest as a career?

Yes _____   No _____   **If yes, which ones?**

_____

_____

_____

_____

Note: If you struggled making a list of interests today, maybe you need a few days to ponder this. Clip articles from magazines or take pictures of things that interest you. Come back and include those items in the list you started here. After a little time, review these things that stimulated you. Think about careers within these areas of interest and try to identify what might work for you.

Now make a list of your areas of interest and prioritize them in order of importance.

_____

_____

_____

_____

_____

_____

Personal Notes

3.2. Talents

After greeting Joe, Paul said, "Joe, I want to introduce you to another cornerstone on which to build your future—your talents. Do you believe you have any special talents?"

"I can dunk a mean basketball, if that's what you mean."

"That's great, but I'm thinking on a somewhat broader scale. A talent is a special, innate ability or aptitude to perform a particular task well. Everyone has unique talents—skills that come naturally and can satisfy your emotional and/or physical needs. For example, a talent for playing a musical instrument can satisfy your desire to create and hear beautiful music—an emotional satisfaction. This same talent might also be used to provide beautiful music for others to enjoy, creating a means to earn a living—a physical objective. Does this discussion help open your mind regarding how a talent might enrich your life?"

"Sort of, but I've never really thought much about talents."

"That's okay, Joe. Most people don't realize the potential importance of their talents because they don't believe they can apply their talents to create significant value in their lives. Is this where you are, Joe?"

"I guess so. Help me understand more about talents from your perspective."

"Many people can perform specific tasks quite well, but most are satisfied with the easy results they can create. They are not driven to achieve a higher level of performance wherein their talent becomes an integral part of who they are. This extra step requires intensive focus and hard work but can create rewards that are absolutely amazing."

"So even though something comes naturally, you're saying it takes time and effort to become really good at it."

"Yes, and there's another element that many people miss. To become great at something requires more than just honing a skill. It requires truly putting your heart into what you do. Your heart is what makes the expression of your talent stand out and touch people memorably. Let me give you a couple of examples:

"Through all the years you attend school, there may be one teacher you remember. One special teacher in my life, Bert, taught high school history. In my experience, history classes generally involved specific facts: when and where particular events took place and the names of people associated with each event. However, Bert enabled his students to feel that they had experienced historical events and understand why those happenings were important. He didn't just convey facts. He put his heart into making them come alive. Many years later, I still remember his teaching. He had a heart for helping his students experience history.

"Similarly, if you put your mind and heart into using your talents, you will stand out from the crowd, Joe. You will make a difference in people's lives, and they will remember you.

"Lenny Sue also expresses her talent with a lot of heart. She is an inspiring, passionate woman. This small, beautiful, unassuming woman is warm and nurturing. Being with her feels like a comforting hug, the unconditionally accepting hug you would get from your mother. She is simply an amazing woman. Her talent/passion/journey didn't give her solid direction until she met a midwife, a visiting speaker at her college. After that, she realized that she had an interest in home birth and began her journey to becoming a passionate midwife who helped women give birth at home. She gave birth to all her own children at home, and she herself has now helped over four hundred babies come into this world.

"She is passionate about her calling. It really is a calling; she is on call 24/7, and she sacrifices much to help women and families according to her philosophy. She believes that women were made to give birth, and she helps create a safe way to allow birth to happen. Because her desire is to serve women in preparation for and during the birthing process, she has spent years developing the required skills and in education/certification studies to become a licensed midwife. There are technical and clinical aspects to pregnancy and birth in addition to the personal aspects of listening and caring. Another talent of hers is being a motherly, nurturing woman: gentle and loving but firm. She is passionate about helping women and their babies. She uses her talent to bless others and makes a very big impact on the families she serves.

"Joe, when you truly apply your heart to using a talent, you will make an impact on other lives! That impact is a natural byproduct of your efforts. It should be exciting to consider the impact you might have. Even if your impact is small in a global sense, it can be large in the lives of others. Do these examples help you understand how your talents can become foundational in your life?"

"I think I'm beginning to see what you mean, but I've never thought about how significant a talent might be."

Stop. Think. Apply.

Recognize Your Individuality

Talents

Summary

- While a talent is usually an innate ability to perform a specific task well, it takes years of dedicated effort to hone a talent into a well-developed skill.
- Applying your heart to the use of your talent is the key to creating something significant in this world—something you and other people will value.
- Be sensitive to how much you enjoy using your talents. A talent can grow into a passion, perhaps even a new career.

Application

Make a list of the talents you believe you possess.

_____
_____
_____
_____

What talents do you prefer/enjoy most?

_____
_____
_____
_____

Why do you feel this is so?

_____
_____
_____
_____

How could you use your talents to create deep joy for yourself and maybe provide something other people can appreciate and value?

_____

_____

_____

_____

A talent can be your ticket to significant purpose. With this in mind, would you be willing to invest time and effort to develop a particular talent of yours into a honed skill?

Yes _____   No _____

Why?

_____

_____

_____

_____

Review what you have written regarding your talents, make a list of the most significant talents you believe you have, and prioritize them in order of their importance to you.

_____

_____

_____

_____

Personal Notes

3.3. Dreams

"Joe, how are you enjoying the discovery process regarding your unique individuality?"

"I've always known I'm a little different from other people, but I never considered what truly makes me different. I'm beginning to understand how my interests and talents may be important, and I feel like I'm peeling an onion, layer by layer. I'm wondering what's coming next."

"It sounds like some lights are turning on within you."

"That's a good way to put it—lights turning on and letting me see what has been there all along, but I never recognized it."

"Let's peel an additional layer off and reveal another cornerstone of your life. One of life's most exciting experiences is to have a deep desire – or a personal dream – come true. Most people, however, don't have such a dream, so they can never experience the great joy of having one come true. Tell me, Joe, do you have a dream regarding your future?"

"Sometimes I dream about improving handicapped people's quality of life. Finding success with such an endeavor might provide a nicer lifestyle for my family. These ideas, however, seem so far from reality that I try not to think about them too much."

"I understand, Joe. Some people call such thoughts daydreams and try to encourage those who do it to snap back to reality because they believe such thoughts are unrealistic."

"My wife tells me that all the time."

"I may understand her concern. Some people spend a lot of time dreaming of changes they desire and even spend a lot of money trying to make that difference happen, but they never accomplish anything significant. So they end up broke. Your wife probably wants to protect you from such behavior."

"I hadn't thought of that, but it makes sense. I certainly don't want to spend all our money chasing my dreams. But what if a dream of mine is truly valuable? How can I know if my idea is good or not?"

"That's a good question, Joe. If you have a truly revolutionary idea with apparent potential to create great impact in people's lives, and it persists in your mind, you want to explore it to determine how it might be developed. Recognize that every technological advancement we have today started in someone's mind as a dream, with the question, 'What if?' And your dream of how things might be different could be important too. Therefore, I suggest you share such a dream with someone you trust, someone who can lead you to people who can help you evaluate it. If you feel it is necessary, you can protect your idea by having the people sign a confidentiality/noncompetition agreement before you share your dream in detail. This way you can get valuable guidance before pursuing your idea further."

"That sounds like a good approach, and it will make me think about my dreams from a different perspective."

"I hope you will begin to consider any persistent dreams as possibilities, not just idle thoughts. And I want you to be aware that your life will always be filled with obstacles, so you need to keep your dreams above the obstacles that appear in your way. Obstacles are just challenges you need to overcome to grow as a person, so think of them as growth opportunities, not stumbling blocks."

"I certainly know how problems get in the way of what I want to accomplish, but thinking of them as growth opportunities will be very different."

"Joe, many people are given significant dreams, but relatively few have the confidence to follow through on their inspirations. The human mind is capable of doing far more than most of us ever do with it in our lifetimes, but many people are constrained by their self-imposed limitations. Hopefully you can have the confidence to act on the creative power you have within you. It can be a highly fulfilling experience, perhaps providing purpose and potentially great rewards."

"I'm excited to know it is okay to dream about possibilities. I've always been told such thoughts were a waste of time, but now I see them in a very different light."

"Good! Now I want you to think about what we have covered today and see if you can identify the dreams you have had over time. List any that have recurred or seemed significant in the following STA section. Include as much information regarding these dreams as you can. Have you asked yourself, 'What if?' If so, make a note of it. Let your mind run free on this exercise, Joe, with no constraints. Like your lists for interests and talents, your list of dreams can help define your individuality."

Stop. Think. Apply.

Recognize Your Individuality

Dreams

Highlights

- Dreams are good! They can open your mind to new purposes in your life.
- Not everyone has the dreams you have. They are part of your uniqueness.
- The movers and shakers of the world all started out with a dream.
- Ask yourself, "What if I could change the future?"

Application

Describe any persistent dreams you have had over time. If you have had thoughts and visions that made you ask the question, "What if?" you should pay special attention to them. Let your mind run free, with no limits, regarding what might be possible. Document as much detail as you can.

_____

_____

_____

_____

Now specifically ask yourself, "What if I could _____?"

_____

_____

_____

_____

Truly believe that anything is possible! You could be the special person who produces a great advance in this world, perhaps one that could greatly improve how people live. Think intently about it! Why not you?

After pondering this question, write down your thoughts and feelings.

_____

_____

_____

_____

What are your most significant dreams?

_____

_____

_____

_____

Personal Notes

3.4. Passions

"Joe, I've been thinking about you dealing with your dreams. How has this gone for you?"

"Very interesting. I've been over a lot of ground, discovered more dreams than I realized I had, and am still trying to figure out what is most significant. You gave me a huge challenge."

"I thought it might be challenging. Most people don't take dreams seriously. People tend to think they are just fleeting fantasies and encourage you to live in reality. Most people don't understand that new, innovative ideas always start as someone's dreams, and the people who seriously consider *What if ...?* are the ones who are later honored as great innovators."

Joe thought for a few seconds, and then responded, "I never thought of it that way. You mean that if I come up with a great idea, I may become famous?"

"I wouldn't go that far yet. You're just beginning to understand the concept of how a dream can develop into something of value. Have you identified a particular dream you want to share with me?"

"Not yet. I'm still trying to sort out my thoughts."

"That's okay, but I want to introduce you to something that will drive a significant dream to reality: passion. Let me explain. A passion is a powerful and compelling emotion, a driving force that can move you forward to accomplish a particular objective. A passion renders all excuses powerless and helps you overcome every obstacle that comes your way. Passion is the fuel that enables you to fulfill your dream and create your desired reality. Passion is what turns you on!"

"Gee, Paul, that sounds awfully powerful. I don't know if I have that kind of power within me."

"I believe you have more than you recognize. You just haven't had anything strong enough to focus on yet. Let me explain how a passion develops.

"You may have an interest in something that drifts along for an undefined period of time because your priorities and time are focused elsewhere. But somewhere along the way your interest—and a dream—may become more significant, and your priorities can change. You can feel the desire for a new focus with an intensity that consumes most of your thoughts and ignites your emotions. When this happens, you have developed a passion.

"Wait a second, Joe. I recall a passion you've had—your boat. Remember when you decided to purchase a boat? You may have spent months researching boats until you found what you wanted. You thought about boats, talked about boats, and finally purchased your own boat. You had a passion for a boat! Am I right?"

"Yes, that's a good example! You're right. I did have a passion for a boat."

"Joe, do you remember how nothing could have stopped you from getting a boat? You need to clarify your most significant dream so you can get that same intensity of feeling again."

"I like the sound of that, Paul, but don't know how to make it happen."

"That's where I come in. My job is to help you clearly define your dream, find the passion to achieve that dream, and discover an intense purpose for your life."

"That sounds too easy. I don't see how I can go from where I've been all my life to such an idealistic place with intense purpose."

"I understand. Where you are headed is very different from the way you have lived thus far. Like you, a lot of people are afraid to dream big dreams because they don't believe they are worthy of achieving them. They protect themselves from disappointment by not getting their hopes up. But little dreams don't require passion because they are too easy to achieve, and they can't create real purpose for you. You are worthy of great achievements, Joe, and I want to encourage you to stretch yourself with a big dream, fuel it with unbridled passion, and discover a real purpose for your future.

"I'd like you to identify the things that turn you on, occupy your thoughts, and stir excitement within you. Think of it this way: get past the things you desire and identify the things you can't live without! I want you to identify the things you absolutely *need*. These are the things in your life that involve passion. Make a list of them in the following STA."

"You talk as if I can do almost anything, Paul."

"You really can. Joe, you need to realize, however, that passion is not passive and internal. While passion may start in your mind and emotions, it drives purposeful action to produce amazing results. Passion is a strong motivator and demands action, but you must have a plan and work your plan to achieve the results you seek. We will get into making your plan of action a little later, but first consider the following examples of people who have had strong passions.

"Consider Judy. When Judy was very young, she became interested in ice skating. She was an ambitious girl, so she worked with a coach to develop her skills and become competitive. She got up early each day for a workout before school, and after school she had another workout, a longer one, before going home for dinner and her homework. This routine defined her daily life until she completed high school, greatly limiting her free time and social interaction with her peers. With continued success, Judy's passion for winning grew, and she decided she wanted to qualify for the Olympics. Her passion drove her to work hard, qualify, compete, and bring home Olympic medals.

"While Olympic competition isn't for everyone, whatever you decide you want to accomplish will require some degree of passion to make it reality. Without passion, people give up on their dreams and accept adequacy as a standard. It's sad to contemplate—our world is full of people who have wanted something better for themselves but have not had passion to bring their dreams into reality.

"Also consider Andy. As a young boy, Andy was excited by the thought of being a fireman. A lot of boys dream about being heroes and saving people from burning buildings. For many, though, this is a fleeting dream. Andy, however, continued to have this desire during his teenage years. He had always been athletic and participated in sports, so he became physically fit. Eventually his interest developed into a passion, so he applied to become part of his local fire department and was accepted into their training program. Since Andy was naturally ambitious, his passion for the job, combined with his desire to be a good leader, resulted in a series of promotions. The difference between Andy's performance and that of others in the department was his passion for the work he did. Passion drives people to seek and attain greater performance than those without passion can ever accomplish. Andy truly found a purpose for his life.

"And then there's Francis. Francis lives in a way that many people wouldn't have the courage to live even if they wanted to do so. He certainly didn't always know he wanted to hike in every country of the world. He started out going to school and earned an MBA from Harvard. He worked in Silicon Valley and had heard about backpacking in the wilderness. He decided he wanted to try it. He researched it, prepared for it, and went on many hikes before hiking the Appalachian Trail. This started out as a simple interest. No one could have predicted the passion that sparked within him.

"His experience on the Appalachian Trail inspired him. He needed to do more. Since then he has done the Pacific Rim Trail, hiked the entire length of the Continental Divide (in both directions), hiked across Spain twice, and backpacked in Europe over several years. He has done an epic journey: hiking through all fifty-four countries in Africa. You can read about Francis Tapon's adventures at www.francistapon.com.

"Francis is so passionate about hiking and his dream of hiking through all the countries of the world that one can't avoid being excited when around him. He loves hiking. He loves meeting people. He loves experiencing nature as well other cultures. His passion for these activities inspires other people as well.

"Francis is doing what he is absolutely passionate about: hiking the world. Hiking might not be considered a talent by some, but hiking as a living is certainly something special! To pay for his passion, he has tapped into his writing skills as well as his sense of humor. Francis has written books on his travels. His books provide funds for his travels and enable him to share his passion with others.

"Francis's story shows how interests and talents can become dreams and passions. His passions ultimately created a purpose for his life. He has produced a television show based on his African travels to inspire others, even if they don't go hiking across Africa themselves.

"Joe, every individual is made with a measure of greatness inside, waiting for us to fuel it with passion. Our passions can create positive changes in the world! For example, consider the people who founded electronic companies in Silicon Valley. They all started by following a dream, but without passion they would never have achieved such great success."

Reader, follow your passion! It can become your purpose.

Stop. Think. Apply.

Recognize Your Individuality

Passions

Highlights

- Passion turns you on! It drives purposeful action to produce amazing results.
- Stretch yourself with a big dream and fuel it with unbridled passion.
- Don't tiptoe through your days. Instead, walk with purpose and enthusiasm.
- Attack your life with passion, and you can find the purpose you seek.

Application

Get ready for what's next!

Define your ideal life. What does it look like?
Write down what you want it to be. Define it in detail so you can feel what it would be like to live that way. Don't hold back; you may discover your purpose in what you write down here.

_____

_____

_____

_____

Set your soul on fire!
Your passion will be specific to you.
Evaluating your personal interests, talents, and dreams, you should have an inkling of where to find your passion. However, if you still feel lost about your passion, consider what your life would be like if money were no object.

What would you want to do with your time every day? How would you choose to change or influence the world? Your passions can give purpose to your life!

Make a list of things that fire you up. Then prioritize them according to their importance to you.

_____

_____

_____

_____

Personal Notes

3.5. A Foundation for Your Future

"Joe, we've covered a lot of ground. We started by defining what has made you who you are today, your: personality, relationships, and experiences. In the STA's you have identified the cornerstones on which to build your future—your interests, talents, dreams, and passions. This is your life we are talking about, and it is your responsibility to define your most significant dream and fuel it with passion to fulfill your purpose. No one else can or will do it for you. Joe, you may never have heard that you can make your life what you want it to be, but it's time for you to hear it. No matter what your life has been to this point, you can truly create your personal dream and discover your purpose in life.

Every new day really is the first day of the rest of your life."

Stop. Think. Apply.

Recognize Your Individuality

A Foundation for Your Future

In the STA's of the prior chapters, you have listed your interests, talents, dreams, and passions. Now put all four cornerstones in place to see the foundation for your ideal future. Yes, this foundation is uniquely your own, so create it with much thought and consideration for your feelings regarding each cornerstone.

Interests   **Priority**

_____   _____

_____   _____

_____   _____

_____   _____

_____   _____

Talents   **Priority**

_____   _____

_____   _____

_____   _____

_____   _____

_____   _____

Dreams   **Priority**

_____   _____

_____   _____

_____   _____

_____   _____

_____   _____

Passions   **Priority**

_____   _____

_____   _____

_____   _____

_____   _____

_____   _____

This chart establishes a foundation for you to use in making future decisions, so make sure you have created it accurately. It is also intended as a guide to help you find your purpose.

Using your foundation as a guide, write down any thoughts and feelings that can help you find your personal purpose.

_____

_____

_____

_____

Personal Notes

Heads up!

Switching Gears!

You have arrived at the heart of this book! The prior sections were to give you foundational information on these topics:

- how your personality, relationships, and experiences have formed you into who you are today
- the key aspects of your individuality that make you different from everyone else in this world: your interests, talents, dreams, and passions, which form the foundation on which you will build the life you want to live and help you find purpose

The rest of this book was written to help you discover the keys to a meaningful purpose. To complete these sections, you will need to dedicate some time to think deeply about who you are as an individual, including an understanding of your inner needs and how you want to live the rest of your life.

Despite what your life has been to this point in time, what you do from here, starting today, could help you find a purpose beyond anything you have imagined.

This may be one of the greatest challenges you ever face, but what will a life driven by purpose be worth to you?

Don't miss it!

Hang onto hope.

Believe in yourself.

And don't forget to smile during this process because you really are headed for a better life! Plan on it. Look forward to it. Expect it to happen!

4. Discover New Possibilities

4.1. Break Out—Discover Freedom

Paul began by saying, "Today I want to introduce you to a couple of concepts that will help you in the rest of our work together. These are keys to discovering a purpose that will allow you to become all you are meant to be."

"Whoa! With a statement like that, you have my attention."

"Good! I need to have you with me on this, because everything we will cover from here on depends on your grasping these principles and applying them to your life. Like many things that are important, the principles are very simple, but many people miss them.

"The first principle is, 'Develop an inquiring mind. Think out of the box.' Seek to explore new and even unconventional ideas and new ways to apply familiar ideas. To recognize significant opportunities, you have to live by this principle, which is something many people never learn to do."

"Paul, I've heard the expression *out of the box* before, but I don't know what it means. Can you help me understand it?"

"Sure. Many people develop routines. They get up, go to work, and after work, they either head home or to some activity they do on a regular basis. These routines become habits, so they follow the same patterns year in and year out. This lifestyle is referred to as *the box*. Have you experienced anything like this?"

"Now that you describe it, yes. My life has followed a regular pattern for years, and as I think about it, this is why I came to you for help."

"I'm not surprised. The important point is that you must be open to new ideas that will provide opportunities for a purposeful future."

"That makes sense, but how do I change how I live, and where do these new ideas come from? My family is used to my routines, and I have to provide income to support our lifestyle."

"I understand, and seeking a way to change your life can be a bit overwhelming. However, you have identified your interests, talents, dreams, and passions, and you've prioritized them. Let them lead you out of your box.

"Joe, the second principle recognizes that, while people tend to get stuck in regular routines, almost everyone has a deep desire for some degree of freedom. How each individual defines freedom can vary widely, and I encourage you to consider this seriously and decide what it means for you as an individual.

"The second principle is to seek personal freedom—a consciousness deep within yourself, guiding you to choose what you will do each day to grow into all you are meant to be. Such an endeavor involves your mind, gut feelings, and discernment. You have control over your thoughts, but they can be influenced by your emotions. Your gut feelings are often your most reliable compass, and discernment comes from personal experience and wise counsel.

Understand that this freedom requires truly knowing who you are and whom you seek to become. Unfortunately, many people never grasp this concept.

"People can have a difficult time defining their visions of personal freedom because they look outside themselves to define what they seek. They blame their lack of freedom on other people, time limitations, the physical world around them, laws governing society, and any other handy excuse. The real problem, however, is usually tied to an emotional outlook or rigid mindset that can block their perspectives so that they do not see the opportunities all around them. As a result, people can place arbitrary constraints on themselves because of their past experiences, fear of failure, or self-doubt. This is a very debilitating box that prevents people from experiencing personal freedom.

"You need to commit to breaking out of the box that has controlled your life!"

Stop. Think. Apply.

Discover New Possibilities

Break Out—Discover Freedom

Highlights

- If your life has been controlled by old patterns, don't let it stay that way.
- Be open. Think beyond your box to find new opportunities.
- Your interests, talents, dreams, and passions are keys to your future.
- Freedom to become all you can be comes from within you.

Application

How would you describe your current life?

Predictable _____ Boring _____ Interesting _____ Exciting _____

Explain:

_____

_____

_____

_____

Could you describe your life as one lived in a box? Yes _____ No _____

Explain what you mean.

_____

_____

_____

_____

Would you like your life to be different? If so, describe the difference(s) you would like.

_____

_____

_____

_____

Referring to your interests, talents, dreams, and passions, what stands out to you as important keys to your future?

_____

_____

_____

_____

How would you define what you desire as your own personal freedom?

_____

_____

_____

_____

If you have any experiences, past failures, or self-doubt holding you back from experiencing personal freedom, list them here.

_____

_____

_____

_____

Do you truly want to leave these things in your past so you can discover your own personal freedom? Yes _____ No _____
Why?

_____

_____

_____

_____

If "Yes," describe how you will leave these things in your past and move forward.

_____

_____

_____

_____

Personal Notes

A Caution!

What You Do Affects Others

What you do affects others because your life doesn't happen in a vacuum. It is essential that you understand this concept and make your effect on others a positive one. You are embarking on an amazing journey that may involve big changes and shifts in your paradigms. It is critical to share this journey with your partner (if you have one) literally every step of the way.

Your relationships are critical to your purpose and personal fulfillment. If you do not have your relationships in order, your full happiness and your greater effectiveness will suffer.

If your personal relationship is currently suffering, you will struggle with moving forward. Moving forward should enrich both of your lives, but just like anything worthwhile, it takes work and dedication. Having that dedication requires you to have your partner on the same page. Or, at the very least, your partner needs to accept that you want to change even if she/ he doesn't fully understand. Sharing your dreams and your goals will help, but it isn't magic. People are people, and change is scary.

What can you do?

1. Seek help. Relationships are wonderful, but they do require work, and sometimes a relationship needs outside help. Find a counselor, a therapist, or a pastor who can work with both of you as a couple.
2. Read *Love & Respect* by Dr. Emerson Eggerichs [5] as well as *The 5 Love Languages* by Gary Chapman [6]. Encourage your partner to read them as well. (Hey, even if you believe you have a great relationship with your partner, these are excellent books to read. If you are not in a relationship but hope to be in one someday, read these books!)
3. Make time for your partner regularly. Life can be hectic, but you need to make sure your partner knows that she/he is a priority to you. (This can tie into *Love Languages*, so it's really important!)

Even if you have a wonderful set of relationships, I encourage you always to strive to be a better person, citizen, parent, and partner. Lifelong personal growth is a wonderful thing!

Western culture says you can achieve success by accumulating money, power, and possessions, but what good are they if you have miserable relationships? Keep your priorities straight, and you will find far greater purpose and personal fulfillment!

4.2. Define Your Priorities

Paul opened the session. "Joe, your personal priorities strongly affect how you make decisions. This is important because the urgencies of life can easily take your focus off what is truly important. Therefore, it is necessary to identify your important priorities, write them down, and keep them readily available to remind you to stay on track.

"Gale Sayers, a former pro football great, defined his priorities this way: 'The Lord is first, my friends are second, and I am third.'[7] While not specifically mentioned in this short quote, Gale's family ranked first among his friends, a place of honor. He knew that keeping his family as a high priority helped him maintain a healthy personal balance. Gale placed himself at the bottom of his priority list, a decision based on his love for and commitment to those he placed more highly. His self-respect didn't suffer, however, as evidenced by how he excelled in his career. His credo provides excellent focus for anyone's life, but you have to choose your own priorities.

"Notice, Joe, that Gale didn't list his career as one of his top priorities. He placed it within his third category—a factor that related to him personally. There's a lesson here: If you have placed your work at a higher priority than your family, you need to reevaluate your priorities—and fix them! Your employer may tell you to put your job as your highest priority, but this will never satisfy all of your inner needs."

"Paul, I've had priorities in my life and tried to keep them straight, but that's all I've done. I have never written them down, so they have been somewhat flexible. And my priorities have been different from Gale's. I like his advice, and I will change my worldview accordingly."

"Don't feel badly. That's the way most people live their lives. It's not really effective, is it?"

"No, it isn't. Having clear priorities will help me determine why I need to place greater importance on some areas and less on others."

"Now write down your top priorities, Joe, along with your deepest thoughts and feelings about them. If you just try to remember your priorities, they won't stick because daily business will get in the way, and you won't remember them or your deepest thoughts and feelings about them. Put your priorities where you will read them every day! These priorities will be determining factors regarding how you make decisions, so make sure you really mean it when you say they are your most important priorities."

Stop. Think. Apply.

Discover New Possibilities

Define Your Priorities

Highlights

- Own your top priorities emotionally and always take care of them first. Other matters that may want your attention can wait.
- Read your priorities often, preferably daily, until they become an integral part of who you are.
- Don't let the urgencies of life interfere with your priorities. Just because something seems urgent at the moment doesn't mean it is truly important.

Application

We all have priorities that affect how we live. Some may change from time to time, depending on what is happening to us.

The priorities we are addressing here, however, are very different from the ones you may think of first. Once these are in place, they don't change for the rest of your life! Using Gale Sayers's priorities as an example of permanent priorities, what are your top priorities?

My Top Priorities:

_____

_____

_____

_____

_____

_____

_____

Why These are Important to Me:

_____

_____

_____

_____

_____

_____

_____

Look at how you have been living. Does it fit with the priorities you just wrote down? If not, how do you need to correct your life to match your new priorities?

_____

_____

_____

_____

Who can you turn to as a mentor to hold you accountable for these lifelong priorities?

_____

_____

_____

_____

Personal Notes

4.3. Listen to Your Gut

As Joe sat down in Paul's office, he started the session. "So, Paul, I have a grasp of the four cornerstones, have defined my top priorities, and would like to have personal freedom. I'm excited to explore possible careers where I can be more fulfilled. How do we start defining my options?"

"Hold on, Joe. We have a lot more to cover before you start trying to identify your next career move. You need to open your mind to a much broader horizon. It's great that you are beginning to gain some insights into who you really are. It can be difficult to change your way of thinking or an approach ingrained from youth. Now I want to help you understand the concept of your inner needs. These are centered in your gut, and you need to understand them."

"I'm guessing you will define what you mean by *inner needs*, right?"

"Of course, Joe."

"I'm ready. Let's go!"

"Good. While everyone has unique needs that are quite personal, there are some needs that are common to all of us. As human beings, we have both emotional and rational natures, and our inner needs come from these roots.

"First, we need a sense of security, of being loved. We were created to be social beings, interacting with other people to have this need met. When this need is truly fulfilled, we will experience comfort, joy, and peace and will generally be happy. This is the way we are intended to live, so be open to people with whom you can share your life to experience fulfillment of this deep need within you.

"If this inner need is not met, people may seek other ways to find personal fulfillment. Some people immerse themselves in their careers, hobbies, possessions, or investments to find a sense of security. Others virtually check out of life and seek isolation, relying entirely on their own resources to provide some degree of personal satisfaction. I don't believe any of these tactics can truly meet our inner need for security.

"Second, we all need a sense of purpose. Far too many people never discover a significant purpose, and that is why I took you through the foundational exercises to determine:

- who you are today and what has made you this way
- what makes you a truly unique individual

"Such perspective should begin to help you discover a purpose that fits your individuality. Realize, however, that you must apply yourself to this purpose with deep commitment and perseverance to realize your full potential.

"The third inner need is hope for the future. Hope can be defined as having confident trust, with total expectation of fulfillment. A powerful motivator, hope will cause you to act decisively, knowing you will experience your desired results. Hope makes no allowance for doubt.

"Most people want more in their futures than they have experienced in their pasts. Their desires may include more personal achievement, happiness, discretionary time, personal freedom, money, close friends... and the list can go on. The core issue for most people is this: what can really provide hope for a better future? Wishful daydreaming certainly can't do it.

"Nothing can or will give you reason to hope for a better future until you change something within yourself. Remaining stuck in the same old habits won't change anything. However, deciding to change your thoughts and actions to produce the future you want can enable you to hope that it will truly happen. Then, as you experience progress toward your goal, you will reinforce your hope and create increased energy and focus to make it happen.

"These inner needs will motivate and drive you. They are the principal components that make up your personal reservoir of fulfillment. You may also have your own personal inner needs that will drive you. You need to become aware of them too. The more you satisfy your inner needs, the fuller your reservoir will be. The fuller you keep your reservoir, or at least the more consistently you fill it, the more overall satisfaction and peace you will find. Are you following?"

"Sure. Can I simply focus on filling one particular inner need at a time?"

"Simple answer: no. You probably will not feel complete by focusing on just one inner need. Your personal fulfillment reservoir involves all your inner needs, so it is important to maintain a healthy balance as you work to keep your reservoir filled.

"I find that a person's inner needs are often satisfied through focused activities. You will find a list of possible inner needs activities in the following STA section. To help you prioritize these activities, I want you to consider this famous scenario: You have a pile of sand, a pile of small stones, and a pile of large stones. They all need to be put into a big jar. Some smart person somewhere has calculated that you can get all three into the jar. How do you do it?"

Joe almost jumped off the sofa. "I know this one! You put in the large stones, and then you put in the small stones. You shake the jar a bit to make them settle, and then you add the sand. You probably should shake the jar some more to make the sand settle all the way to the bottom, but you can get all these items into the jar. It's a fun exercise I saw in college. One student put the sand in first, then the small stones, and then couldn't fit all the large stones into the jar."

"I'm glad you have this visual! It will be great for determining the real importance of your various activities. Put your main focus on the activities that best support your inner needs. These are represented by the large stones. Big things always come first! This will also help your reservoir feel fuller faster.

"The small stones represent activities of slightly lower priority. As you truly think about these activities, however, you may be surprised to find one or two that significantly help satisfy an inner need. This can be an important revelation and may cause you to revise the priorities you place on your activities.

"The sand represents activities of the lowest priority. There are two points you should address regarding these particular activities: Does an item on this list help support an inner need in some subtle way? If an item on this list is of marginal value, should you drop it?

"I want you to remember this stone/sand concept when setting priorities in other aspects of your life as well. Take some time to think hard about your inner needs. I've included a list of potential activities that might help you, but it is by no means exhaustive. This is just to get your wheels turning and get you thinking. It's okay if you also need to start broadly and drill down to something more specific. And, Joe, some activities might fuel more than one inner need. Highlight these."

"Paul, this sounds like an important subject—something I've never thought about. Thank you for your guidance."

Stop. Think. Apply.

Discover New Possibilities

Listen to Your Gut

Highlights

- You have a reservoir for your inner needs. This needs to be kept relatively full to optimize your sense of peace and satisfaction.
- These inner needs are often the motivations that cause you to act.
- Understanding how to satisfy your inner needs is critical to your personal fulfillment.

Application

In addition to the needs common to most people -- sense of security, sense of purpose and hope for the future -- my personal inner needs include:

_____

_____

_____

_____

Inner Needs Activities

List activities you believe can help keep your inner needs reservoir full. Make it exhaustive.

The following is just a list of suggestions to help you get started. Please add anything to this list that seems appropriate for you as an individual.

raise and support a loving family
serve/protect others
care for people/animals/nature
defend our country
act as part of a team
solve problems/challenges
create art/music
original thoughts (discovery)
make the world a better place
plant and care for a garden

share life with someone special
accumulate personal wealth
create value/positive change in lives
own a business
comfort/fit in with other people
maintain good health/conditioning
have control (be in charge)
educate people
achieve goals/be competitive

Add more activities that help satisfy your inner needs here.

_____

_____

_____

_____

This is where you choose activities that will help satisfy your inner needs.

List your large stones.

_____   _____

_____   _____

_____   _____

List your small stones.

_____   _____

_____   _____

List the sand that you want to keep.

_____   _____

_____   _____

Write the appropriate letter next to each activity as follows: S (security); P (purpose) H (hope); M=my own.

If you find an inner need that is not supported, you need to review your activities and revise your assessment.

This list is for your life, so give this exercise the time and effort it deserves!

Personal Notes

4.4. Never Work a Day in Your Life

"Joe, I hope you see how your gut can be a powerful guide in your life," said Paul, "because it knows you very well and will lead you on a path that is good for you."

"I've never thought of my gut as a guide in my life, but it does talk to me at times and gives me feelings that influence some of the choices I make."

"Good. I'm glad you get it, and I encourage you to use your gut as one of the most important sources of guidance in your life. Now I want to introduce you to a concept that most people don't understand. Because they don't, they think of what they do to earn a living as just a job they have to do every day. Life doesn't have to be this way!

"I'd like you to use your understanding of who you are and what makes you a unique individual to discover what lifestyle can enable you to provide for your family while fulfilling your inner needs. This concept is very different from just finding a job to earn a paycheck.

"I like the way Ron Daniels [4] puts it. He says, 'Do what you love to do, and you will never work a day in your life.' This may sound a bit idealistic, but it really can be achieved by anyone who takes this advice seriously. The key to this type of success is identifying a career that fits who you are as an individual by meeting your personal inner needs. Ron, for example, earned a master's degree in mathematics but discovered and joined (and is now president of) his brother's business, which designs and builds imaginative, playful structures for individuals and businesses around the world.

"Ron is a good example of someone who thinks outside of the box, and enjoys his life far more than the average person. You may not see yourself as someone this unconventional, but I encourage you to stretch yourself. You never know where such mental freedom can take you. It doesn't matter if you want your own firm or are happy working in someone else's business. Determine how you want to use your mind and body and be true to who you are as an individual."

"I never realized such a thing was possible. Please help me learn to have that in my life."

"I believe the following questions will help you apply what you have learned about yourself to a search for a good career choice."

Note to the reader: This is your time to dream expansively, so let your thoughts and feelings run free. There are no limits to what you put down here. Make the list in STA as long as you want. You probably have never had such an opportunity before, so be true to yourself and learn all you can about what is within you.

Your thoughts and feelings may change in the future, and that's okay, so know you can revisit this exercise any time you wish. You need to write down everything that is true for you right now so you can make the best possible choices at this time.

Stop. Think. Apply.

Discover New Possibilities

Never Work a Day in Your Life

Highlights

- Don't resign yourself to doing a job that makes you miserable.
- Commit time and energy to identify work you really enjoy doing.
- Ultimately, strive to discover what you truly love to do, and "you will never work a day in your life."

Application

Who are you as a person today, and who do you want to become? Why?

_____
_____
_____
_____

What do you need to do to get there?

_____
_____
_____
_____

Do you have the ability to get there—personal qualities, financial resources and other factors? Why do you believe this is true?

_____
_____
_____
_____

Do you like to work alone or as part of a team? Why?

_____
_____
_____
_____

If you would like to work with people, would you like to work with children or adults? Why?

_____

_____

_____

_____

What kind of work environment suits you—an office or outdoors? Why?

_____

_____

_____

_____

Would you like to have a salary or income based on performance? Why?

_____

_____

_____

_____

Do you want every day to be similar, or do you want varied experiences? Why?

_____

_____

_____

_____

Is it important to be home every night, or is some travel of interest? Why?

_____

_____

_____

_____

_____

_____

_____

_____

_____

_____

_____

_____

_____

Is a company-provided retirement plan a requirement for you? Why?

_____
_____
_____
_____
_____
_____
_____
_____
_____
_____
_____
_____
_____
_____
_____
_____
_____

Is living in one general location important, or would you move extensively to follow job opportunities? Why?

_____
_____
_____
_____
_____
_____
_____
_____
_____
_____
_____
_____
_____
_____
_____
_____
_____

What do you love to do so much that you do not consider it work at all? Perhaps you have a hobby that can be developed into a career.

_____

_____

_____

_____

Identify career options that could be of interest to you. Here are some options that might trigger your thoughts regarding possibilities.

Be exhaustive with your input. Add what is important to you.

working with my hands

business processes

solving puzzles (like forensics)

managing people

professional (like law or accounting)

construction (includes all skills)

routine tasks

creative tasks (designing, engineering)

working in an office environment

other interesting options

health care

science/technical

sales/service

working with animals

music/crafts/artisanship

helping people

physical activity

sports/competitive games

working outdoors

_____   _____

_____   _____

_____   _____

_____   _____

_____   _____

Circle everything that possibly applies to you. Now fill in the following chart.

Career of Interest

(Experienced or desired)

What inner need does it satisfy?

(What do you like about it?)

_____   _____

_____   _____

_____   _____

_____   _____

_____   _____

_____   _____

Remember, your inner needs can be some of your strongest motivators!

Prioritize the options you have listed and write the most important ones here.

_____
_____
_____
_____
_____
_____
_____
_____
_____

Now, with your inner needs (sense of security/ being loved, sense of purpose, hope for the future, plus your own individual needs) and cornerstones (interests, talents, dreams, and passions) in mind, write down your thoughts and feelings regarding your selections.

_____
_____
_____
_____
_____
_____
_____
_____
_____

Important Points

- This is your life, so take responsibility for understanding yourself to make wise career choices.
- Factors in your life can change over time, including your circumstances, desires, economic conditions, and current technologies; entire industries come and go. You may want to change careers at a later time, and this is okay. You need to follow your heart. The STA within this chapter may be helpful during such times.
- The life of your dreams isn't going to drop into your lap. You need to think intently about your options and be willing to work toward this objective.
- Seriously consider Ron Daniels' motto for a successful life: "Do what you love to do, and you will never work a day in your life!"

You may be afraid of change, perhaps because of bad experiences in your past.
So I'll say it again: every new day is the first day of the rest of your life!

Personal Notes

4.5. Gain Some Perspective

Paul opened their next discussion by saying, "You've written a list of career options that interest you, Joe. Now you need to learn more about your choices. This is important because things are not always as they seem."

"How do I do that, Paul?"

"You need to get input from as many sources as possible until you develop a clear and concise definition of what you really want to do, based on your individuality, purpose, inner needs, and the information you gather from the following sources."

- **Ask family, friends, and associates for leads.** These are the people who know you best and have an interest in seeing you succeed. Their knowledge and experiences can give you different perspectives on your desires. Some of these people might be very successful, able to guide you in ways you have never considered.

- **Mine the Internet.** Research the types of work you think you would enjoy and determine what types of companies require someone with your experience and skills. Learn what they do and what they look for in the people they hire.

- **Use social networking services.** These sources can provide a broad array of opportunities for you. You can find a wealth of information regarding different careers on LinkedIn, Facebook, Plaxo, Twitter, Craigslist, Indeed, and many more sites.

- **Consult business development organizations.** Most communities have organizations that help individuals and companies explore business development opportunities. These generally require a membership, but they have frequent events where you can meet people with local companies and develop relationships with business leaders in your area.

- **Explore your chamber of commerce.** This organization is dedicated to helping businesses network with other businesses to promote growth opportunities. In addition, some chambers have volunteers who will advise individuals regarding starting businesses and connecting with business leaders.

- **Communicate with people.** People you meet know other people! Actively get to know others, and eventually you will meet influential people through them. Do this online and in person on a daily basis. Develop relationships with these people regarding their interests. When appropriate, seek their guidance regarding your interests. Over time, you will build a significant network of people who can offer advice and guidance.

- **Ask for referrals**. People who know you and care about you can introduce you to people who might provide valuable guidance on a career you haven't even considered. A personal referral can be a powerful introduction to someone you would otherwise never be able to meet.

- **Make personal inquiries.** You can contact appealing companies to see if your interests might apply to their operations. As you pursue this investigative process, you may learn that some of the career options that attracted you are not what you expected. You may also discover new opportunities of greater interest.

"While studying career options, you should also investigate various companies of interest to learn which ones treat their people well and which ones don't. This is important because the company you work for can be as important as the function you perform for them. You may need to reevaluate your objectives, so be open to new options that are more beneficial to your future. "

Overwhelmed, Joe said, "Sounds like a long process. Meanwhile I guess I'm stuck at my current job."

"For now, that is probably best. At least until you really know where you want to go from here. This process will take some time, but the time and effort you put into it will be very worthwhile. You should learn a lot, and this will help you select your next career move more effectively. And you need to keep a journal of all the people you talk with, including the guidance they give you, who they refer you to, your thoughts and feelings regarding their input, and how your objectives might evolve over time."

"Paul, this seems to involve a lot of time and effort, and it's something I would never have thought to do on my own. But it also sounds like I can learn a lot through the process, which might lead me to a career I have never considered."

"This could be one of the most important assignments you will ever have because it can help you find a career that is extremely fulfilling and, perhaps, a purpose beyond your expectations. It can also help you build a network of people you might associate with for the rest of your life."

"This process is a new concept to me, and I see where I might learn a lot from it."

"I look forward to following your progress, so stay in touch."

Stop. Think. Apply.

Discover New Possibilities

Gain Some Perspective

Highlights

- Get out and investigate what you think you want to do. Other people can provide important perspectives regarding possible career options.
- Develop a network of people you know. You never know who might become a good friend and a great source of guidance.
- This is a win for you! You will either confirm what you want to do or discover new options to satisfy your inner needs better and fulfill a significant, personal purpose.

Application

I dare you to take these steps.

- Follow the plan given to Joe in this chapter. You can develop a network of great contacts and you may discover a career that fulfills your inner needs and supports a significant purpose for your life.
- Step out of your comfort zone. Think outside the box. Ask questions to learn more about career options and prospective employers.
- Develop a large network of people who know and care about you. They can become treasured assets.

Follow this plan and keep a log of your investigative activities, including your feelings about what you learn about career opportunities.

_____

_____

_____

_____

Note that this space is intended only as a starting point. You need to create a personal journal as you build your network, making notes regarding every time you meet with each individual.

When the timing is appropriate, transfer the following information from your journal to this page as a summary.

What career options do you seem to like best?

_____

_____

_____

_____

What do you think you want to avoid?

_____

_____

_____

_____

Are you inspired to look deeper into particular opportunities? What are they?

_____

_____

_____

_____

Go for it! There's no downside to investigating career opportunities, and the upside potential can fulfill your inner needs and provide a personal purpose beyond your imagination!

Personal Notes

4.6. Play Hard and Often

As Joe settled in, Paul said, "Joe, I want you to address this section on play time with the open mind I encouraged regarding your career. There are no limits for your inputs, so get in touch with your deepest desires and inner needs."

Laughing, Joe responded, "What 'play time'?"

"Play time is just like it sounds. It's time when you can do anything you want, with anyone or anything of your choice."

"I don't know. That sounds very different from my life."

"It may sound different from your experience, Joe, but you really can create time for recreational activities you want to do. I believe it's important for you to do so. While you need to have a productive career, you also need to schedule play time into your life. It can greatly enhance your career objectives."

"Sounds good, but my life is full now. I don't know how to put more into each day."

"I understand how you feel, and you need to learn to plan your days differently in the future."

"I assume you can help me with that."

"Yup. I'm good at it. I used to be busy all the time, like you, but I learned how to create time for play, and my productivity went up!"

"Say what? You get more done in less time?"

"Yes, every day! And I enjoy my play time each day too."

"Okay, how do I do that?"

"The key is learning to schedule and prioritize your time. Most people have tasks they need to do each day, and they go from one chore to another somewhat systematically. They can get distracted along the way, causing their tasks to take longer than they expected. At the end of each day, they find they have accomplished less than they wanted. Does this ever happen to you, Joe?"

"I hate to admit it, but, yes, all the time."

"It happens to most people, so don't feel badly about it. You can change how you use your time, however, and it's important to identify what you would like to do during your play time. If you want these things badly enough, they will motivate you to create time for them. The way you do this is to schedule both your work time and your play time. Do you think you'd be willing to try this, Joe?"

"Sure, I'd like to have more control over my time. I'm just a little skeptical about making a schedule work. Events in my daily life require me to be flexible, like: my wife or kids getting sick, car problems, work requirements, and other interruptions."

"I understand, but interruptions don't happen every day. I'm talking about normal days, not occasional ones. If you can make a schedule for normal days, it will help you be more effective at work and with your family."

"If I can create that result, I'm willing to try it."

"Then make a schedule for when you need to be at work and when you think you can have an hour or so of play time on a regular basis. I realize you have not been taking time to play in the past, but you need to do it now. Just do it. It will make you more effective at everything else you do. Make a copy of it for both home and work so both you and your family will have it available."

"This is a real change for me, Paul, but I'm willing to try it."

"Good. Know that you can develop new habits that will make your life better. Trust me on this."

Stop. Think. Apply.

Discover New Possibilities

Play Hard and Often

Highlights

- Scheduling play time into your life makes you more productive while you're working.
- Learn to minimize distractions that compromise your schedule.

Application

The following chart requires you to identify the activities you would like to do during your play time. To inspire recreational possibilities, here are some options that might be helpful.

travel	performance (theatre, music)
sports (individual or team)	enjoy playing with your "toys"
serve people's needs	work with animals/nature
family recreation	create alone (read, paint, write, music, crafts)
specialized cooking	enjoy nature (hiking, scuba diving)
investigating new interests	relaxation, peace, comfort
other personal choices:	

_____   _____

_____   _____

_____   _____

Circle everything that is truly important to you.

Pair your desired play activities with your inner needs they satisfy.

Play-Time Activity	**What inner need does it satisfy?**
(Experienced or desired)	(What do you like about it?)

_____   _____

_____   _____

_____   _____

_____   _____

_____   _____

_____   _____

Now prioritize the items you have listed.

Consider the following points.

- inner needs (sense of security, being loved; sense of purpose; hope for the future, and "my own")
- cornerstones (interests, talents, dreams, and passions)

Write down your thoughts and feelings regarding your play-time selections.

_____

_____

_____

_____

Personal Notes

4.7. A New Day Dawning

Paul opened the day's session by saying, "Now, Joe, I want you to take your top priorities, your top few selections from your inner needs, career options, and play-time lists, plus your cornerstones, and put them all in one place. This composite picture should help you envision how you want to live the rest of your life. This can be a new day dawning for you—when you understand what is truly important in your life and have a tool to help you stay focused to make your future what you want it to be.

"Take time when completing this picture and answering the following questions. They can provide strong guidance to finding your purpose in this world."

Stop. Think. Apply.

Discover New Possibilities

A New Day Dawning

My Top Priorities in Life:

_____
_____
_____
_____
_____
_____
_____
_____
_____
_____
_____
_____
_____
_____
_____
_____
_____
_____
_____
_____
_____
_____
_____
_____

My desired career	fulfills this inner need	and builds on this cornerstone
_____	_____	_____
_____	_____	_____
_____	_____	_____
_____	_____	_____

My desired play-time activity	fulfills this inner need	and builds on this cornerstone
_____	_____	_____
_____	_____	_____
_____	_____	_____
_____	_____	_____
_____	_____	_____

Does anything in this composite picture stand out for you?

_____

_____

_____

_____

Can you begin to understand a significant purpose for your life?
What might it be? List potential options.

_____

_____

_____

_____

How can your desired career and play-time activities help you fulfill such a purpose?

_____

_____

_____

_____

If you see that some compromises might be required, what are they?
How might you optimize your options to support your purpose?

_____

_____

_____

_____

Additionally, have you ever had an idea that could change lives?

_____

_____

_____

_____

Have you felt inspired?

_____

_____

_____

_____

_____

_____

_____

Have you ever wanted something more?

_____

_____

_____

_____

_____

_____

_____

_____

Have you ever wanted to provide something greater?

_____

_____

_____

_____

Have you wanted to change the world?

_____

_____

_____

_____

Have you ever started a question with, "What if ..."?

_____

_____

_____

_____

Our world has been shaped by generations upon generations of people who asked, "What if?" and "What can I do?"

Write down your most significant "what if?" concerns.

_____
_____
_____
_____

Decide what you will do about them and write it here!

_____
_____
_____
_____

Summary statements

- This is your opportunity to find a purpose beyond anything you have ever imagined possible!
- Build your dream with unbridled passion and expect great results!
- Tackle your "what if" questions with courage and do what you are led to do.
- Be excited for your future and make your purpose your reality!

Every new day truly is the first day of the rest of your life!

Personal Notes

5. Make It Happen

5.1. Grow Where You Are Planted

"Joe, as you consider where you might go from here, are you open to some new thoughts?" Paul posed this question at the beginning of Joe's next session.

"Yes, I have new insights into myself, but I have no idea how to apply them to my future."

"I understand your future may not be clear yet, so let's consider your basic options. Either you want to have your own business or you will need to work in someone else's business. Do you have a preference at this time?"

"I think I need to work in someone else's business."

"Then I'd like to give you some wise, farmer-based advice: First, try to grow where you are planted! While you understand your current job very well, there can be many factors that influence your lack of satisfaction. I want you to open your mind a bit. Think about the reputation you have developed with your current employer. Do you think you are respected for the value you bring to the company?"

"Yes, I do. I work hard at my job. I believe I provide a lot of value, and it is appreciated. But I don't feel fulfilled anymore."

"I understand. Recognize there is a lot that happens beyond your job that enables the company to provide products and services to its customers. And within the rest of the company there are probably areas that could benefit from your experience to increase both the company's profits and value in the marketplace.

"I suggest you consider how you might help your current employer in these two areas, perhaps in an entirely different position, before investigating a different firm. Ask leaders within the company, 'Where can I provide value in another part of the company?' You may be very surprised by what you learn."

"Gee, I never thought of approaching them for that kind of discussion. Is that what you mean by thinking beyond the box?"

"It's a good example of the concept. I suggest you talk with your boss and maybe someone in the human resources department concerning what you have been learning about yourself. Tell them you want to provide greater value to the company and to its customers. Avoid just looking to make more money. More money will come as you provide greater value. Does this make sense to you?"

"Yes, it does. I've never thought of talking with people in the company like this."

"I'm sure the company values you as an employee, so they should want to help you make a larger contribution to both the company and its customers. If you don't find a new position that excites you, you can consider looking outside the company for a new job."

Stop. Think. Apply.

Make It Happen

Grow Where You Are Planted

Highlights

- First, consider growing within your current company.
- Build on the reputation and respect you have earned.
- Seek a new position where you can make a larger contribution.

Application

Every company wants to find ways to provide greater value to its customers. That is how it can increase its market share.

As you consider your current employer's operations, look for ways you can provide greater value.

How could you help the company reduce costs to produce products and/or provide services?

_____

_____

_____

_____

How could you help improve the products/services the company offers to provide greater value to customers?

_____

_____

_____

_____

How might you help the company identify new products/services to satisfy needs in the marketplace?

_____

_____

_____

_____

If you were in charge of this company, what could you do to increase profits, create better products/services, and expand the customer base?

_____

_____

_____

_____

Personal Notes

5.2. Seeking New Horizons

Paul began, "Joe, what have you learned in discussions with your current boss and other people in the company?"

"People were surprised that I wanted to investigate ways I could add more value to the company and our customers. I don't think many people talk with them that way. No one had a clear idea where they might use me, but they said they would see what could be arranged."

"I'm not surprised they reacted like that. What you have done is very different for them, but I'm sure they appreciate what you want to do. While you're waiting for them to respond to your request, I'd like to address your desire to investigate other employers. How do you think you might go about such a task?"

"I can learn what other companies do and the kind of people they hire."

"That's a good way to start. You've been working for a fairly large company for a few years and have some good experience. Now you might investigate small and medium-sized companies in addition to other large ones. You might be able to obtain a position with greater responsibility in a smaller company than you could ever find within a large firm. Does this difference seem appealing to you?"

"I certainly like the idea of having a larger scope of work with greater responsibility. Yes, I'd like to explore other options."

"First, you need to write down a description of who you are, what you have accomplished in your career, and the value you can bring to an employer. This becomes your résumé, which you'll send when responding to a company seeking new employees. To create the most effective résumé possible, do some research on the Internet. Templates are available to help you organize your capabilities and experience into polished and readable formats.

"When applying to medium-sized companies, you will have to rely on your résumé to introduce you, but with smaller firms, you can apply in person. And smaller firms might be more willing to fit job functions to who you are as an individual."

"I've never worked in a small company, but you make this environment sound attractive. You are definitely opening my mind to possibilities outside my box."

"Joe, there is something we haven't talked about, and it's important in today's world. Many companies will advertise jobs on the Internet and/or employ headhunters to find employment candidates. You will need to use these resources to notify the world that you are available.

"You should also talk with people you know regarding finding a new job and get referrals to people they know. You may be surprised where this can lead you. Seeking a new job can be interesting and even exciting. You can learn a lot about new industries and new companies and perhaps find a job that is far better than your old one. I'll add one final thought—keep an open mind to opportunities beyond the box."

Stop. Think. Apply.

Make It Happen

Seeking New Horizons

Highlights

- Prepare a résumé that conveys, clearly and concisely, the value you can provide.
- Be open to a variety of company sizes.
- Talk with people you know and get referrals.
- Seek the right fit for yourself and your skills; try to find a job that you would love to do.

Application

Looking for new employment is a job in itself; take it seriously and work at it daily.

New technologies are changing the world at an increasing rate, so approach this task with an inquiring mind.

Stay positive and expect great results!

Make a list of industries that interest you and prioritize them.

_____

_____

_____

_____

Why are you interested in these industries?

_____

_____

_____

_____

Make a list of companies in your most desirable industries.

_____

_____

_____

_____

Identify which companies are most desirable to you.

_____

_____

_____

_____

Do you know people who work in these industries? If you don't know anyone, identify significant people you can call to learn about opportunities within the industries. List these people here.

_____

_____

_____

_____

Do you want to work where you live, or are you willing to move for the right opportunity? List places where you would consider moving.

_____

_____

_____

_____

Personal Notes

5.3. Creating Change

"Joe, you've made great strides toward evaluating who you are today and have some insights into what can bring greater purpose and fulfillment into your life. Now we will begin to define how you can get from where you are today to where you want to be. Are you ready for it?" Paul asked.

"Yes. I need you to guide me through the process, but I'm ready to get started. I'm really excited because I'm starting to see new possibilities for my future," said Joe.

"Good. While other people and events beyond your control have influenced your life in the past, it's time for you to take responsibility for your future. If you honestly want to make your life better, you need to focus on what you *can* control and change. I like how Steven Aitchison [7] puts it: 'I just woke up one day and decided I didn't want to feel like this anymore, or ever again. So I changed. I had lots of excuses for not being able to change, but at the end of the day, they were excuses. Being able to change starts with a decision to change.'"

"Just like that?"

"Yup! You have the power inside you to change your future, and it is just a decision away. Once you make the decision, you have already started the process of creating change. You're either ready to make your life different, or you aren't. "Are *you* ready for change, Joe?"

"I'm ready!"

"Okay, then here we go.

"As a human being, you are gifted with two special attributes. You have the power to reason: the ability to think, analyze, and draw conclusions. And you have free will: the freedom to choose what you will think and do at any point in time.

"Both of these attributes are centered in your thoughts. Whether you realize it or not, Joe, your thoughts control your actions. So the simple answer to making your life better is changing your thoughts. You need to learn to think differently!"

"That sounds way too simple. And, on the other hand, it sounds very hard to do. I've been thinking a certain way all my life, and I don't know how to change that."

"As I related in the example I gave you, if you really want to change your thoughts, you need to decide you're going to do it. That's how it has to start. So I ask you again, Joe, are you ready for this?"

"I'm ready for my life to be different. That's why I came to you. So yes, I'm ready. A little concerned about how to change my thoughts, but I trust you will help me do it."

"While it may seem a little overwhelming right now, you can do this! And once you experience a new way of thinking, you won't want to go back because you will like the direction of your life. Let me ask you, Joe—how do you feel about the concept of your thoughts controlling your actions?"

"That's a completely new concept. Something I've never heard or thought about."

"It may be, but it is very important to your future. I'd like to help you learn how you can control your thoughts. Would that be of interest?"

"Yes. You have my attention."

"You may never have thought about talking to yourself, but people talk to themselves constantly. What you say to yourself is the key to how you think and behave. Joe, you have created patterns of self-talk all of your life, mostly subconsciously, and these patterns tend to strengthen as they persist, reinforcing your behavior patterns over time. However, there is a way to change how you talk to yourself. Would you like more control over your thoughts and your life?"

"Yes!"

"You can have it, so let's get into it. First, I want you to understand that positive self-talk needs to be driven by strong purpose. You need to decide how you want to think and behave. Then talk to yourself in a way that encourages you to conform to your desires. The strength of your purpose will determine your success at changing how you think.

"While the concept is quite simple, at first you will have to catch yourself in the midst of habitual thoughts and consciously tell yourself to think positive thoughts. For example, if you are habitually critical of other people, learn to catch yourself as a critical thought occurs and look for something positive about the person in question. Do this over and over until you don't think of being critical any more. It may take some time to avoid being critical, but you can train your mind to look for positive qualities and create new thought processes and new habits."

"Doesn't sound easy, but if that's what I need to do, I'll do it."

"Another type of self-talk is an affirmation, a statement or proposition you declare to be true. These are effective because your mind will accept anything you tell it to believe without questioning the truth of your input. How's that for control of your thoughts?"

"You mean that all these years, while I have been doubting myself, my mind has been accepting that I might be wrong about issues that matter?"

"If you have been telling yourself that you may need to question your thoughts and decisions, your mind will accept your input and tell you to question yourself. That type of thinking will undermine your self-confidence."

"That's not good news. I tend to rethink all the time."

"I'm glad you now realize how you have been undermining yourself. You can change that habit, starting today, if you want to."

"Now that I know how I defeat myself, I do want to change my self-talk."

"Good! Positive affirmations work immediately. Let me give you an example. In the well-known children's story, 'The Little Engine That Could,' a small engine is pulling a heavily loaded train up a mountain. It knows it has to make it to the top because its cargo is needed on the other side. So the engine tells itself, 'I think I can, I think I can, I think I can.' With this encouragement, the engine pulls harder than it has ever pulled before until it reaches the top of the mountain. Then, on the way down the other side, it repeats, 'I thought I could.' And it smiles all the way to its destination.

"With self-encouragement, the engine believed it could accomplish the difficult task, and it did. You can encourage yourself to accomplish tasks that seem overwhelming too. And this is not a silly concept, Joe, but a proven technique. I dare you to try it. It works!"

"It's really that simple? I just tell myself I can accomplish a difficult task, and I will actually be able to do it?"

"You have to say it to yourself until you truly believe it. Once you believe it, you will put your heart into your endeavor and discover you can do it. Consider another story that supports the power of affirmations.

"A sailboat was out for a day on the ocean, beyond the protection of the San Francisco Bay. When a storm appeared out of nowhere, large waves kept breaking over the boat, causing it to take on water, so the crew radioed an SOS to the Coast Guard. The Coast Guard responded, sending a large cutter to rescue the people on the sailboat. Upon arrival, the cutter captain evaluated the large waves and decided he had to use a smaller boat to rescue the people, lest his boat crush the sailboat in the heavy seas. He had two smaller boats on board, one with a motor and one powered by oars. As he considered his options, he remembered a very important concept: A motor is limited by the power built into it, but committed people do not have such a limitation. Very simply, the crew took the rowboat and willed themselves to pull harder than they ever had before because they knew they were the only hope for the people in trouble on the sailboat. The rescue was successful."

"So it's not just telling myself I can do something. I have to commit to making it happen. Right?"

"Bingo! Commitment involves both your belief level and your heart. There are three steps to this affirmation process: thinking something might be possible and telling yourself you can do it, believing you really can do it, and putting all your effort and heart into it until it is a reality."

"Then I have to become really involved to make it happen. Is that right?"

"Yes. You could do just the first part and have limited effect, but real results come from acting upon your beliefs. Nothing that has real value in this life is easy. Simple, perhaps, but not easy. Joe, I want you to do something to prove to yourself how this process works: Write down a handful of positive thoughts. Look in the mirror and say them to yourself out loud several times a day. It might feel a little silly at first, but I dare you to try it. In time, you will discover you can't help but feel better about yourself! Here are some examples of things you might say: 'I am a winner; I am pleasing to myself and to others; I am intelligent, and I make good decisions.' These are just suggestions. You choose what you want to say to yourself."

"I've never thought of talking to myself out loud, particularly while looking in a mirror, but I will try it. I just have to make sure my family is not watching or listening to me."

"Joe, I encourage you to get very specific with your affirmations. Choose words that resonate for you. You can make it as complicated or as simple as you desire, but keeping it simple might be a good way to start, like 'I am healthy, intelligent, and have great energy.' If you are trying to quit a bad habit, you might say, 'I make healthy choices.' Or perhaps 'Today is a gift, and I will use it wisely.'"

"This is a lot to absorb. I really have to think about all you have covered today so I can use it to change my thoughts."

"Changing your thoughts is critical to changing your life, Joe, so please take this seriously."

"This is all very new for me, so can you give me another example?"

"Sure. One of my clients, Susan, was struggling with self-esteem. She came up with her own affirmation. She kept it simple and easy to remember: 'Slim, strong, and desirable.' She wrote it down five times daily for three weeks. She also repeated it to herself many times a day. She continued to repeat it to herself for months. There may have been days she missed repeating it, but overall she did it faithfully. During this time, she started to feel better about herself. One day she weighed herself and realized that she had lost weight during that time. These thoughts helped her naturally make better choices. This is an example of making your own reality happen by programming your subconscious. And it is your free will that enables you to have control over the process of changing your life the way you desire. You are a walking, talking good deal, Joe. You can provide unique value to this world. For example you can learn to have greater appreciation and love for your family and friends and develop new ways to improve our environment. You might create beautiful music, develop an appreciation for nature, and share it with others. You might help other people with no expectation of anything in return and, yes, discover your ideal career too.

"Joe, I want you to pay special attention to this chapter because it involves much more than just words. It is about personal experiences, habitual thoughts, deep emotions, important decisions, and commitment to act on those decisions—all to create real, meaningful change in your life."

"Why haven't I known any of this before now? I never realized that my thoughts and what I say to myself can actually control how I behave on a daily basis."

"You are just beginning to understand that words have power, so use them wisely in what you say to yourself and to others. A word of caution: Be specific in what you say! I love the story about the man who finds a genie in a bottle and is granted one wish. The man asked for a million bucks. He received a million male deer. The moral of the story: It is important to be specific. Remember to be positive! You get what you focus on! You create your own reality! Be specific!"

Stop. Think. Apply.

Make It Happen

Creating Change

Highlights

- Take responsibility for your future! Creating change in your life starts with a decision to change.
- Your thoughts control your actions, so changing your thoughts is crucial to changing your life.
- What you say to yourself will determine how you think and behave.
- Focus on what you can control and change.

Application

To understand how simple it is to make a significant change in your life, read the words of Steven Aitchison at the beginning of this chapter again. Maybe his recommendation is not an easy one for you to carry out, but it is truly simple.

In line with Steven Aitchison's statement, recognize you can change your life whenever you decide to do it. So when you are ready to change, it is not a hard action to take; you just have to want sincerely to change and decide you will change!

Is there any aspect of your life that you wish were different?
Yes _____ No _____ **If yes, describe and explain that aspect.**

_____

_____

_____

_____

Recognizing that your thoughts and what you say to yourself control how you behave, how would you like to change what you say to yourself and your behavior?

_____

_____

_____

_____

Here are some ways you can change your thoughts—which will create changes in your behavior.

1. **Write a few affirmations here that you would like to be true. Be as specific as possible.**

_____

_____

_____

_____

2. **Now go to a mirror and practice saying these affirmations to yourself five times. Although you have probably never done this, try it! How does this feel?**

_____

_____

_____

_____

This exercise may seem strange at first, but believe you can truly change your thoughts to change your behavior. Just do it!

3. **For those affirmations you wish to internalize, you need to write them down at least five times, several times every day, for three weeks. After this three-week period, continue to write them down once every day until you believe you have internalized them, which will mean that they have become part of you, and you own them.**

During this entire exercise and for as long as you need to do it (until you truly believe these affirmations), say them out loud to yourself in front of a mirror every single day.

I challenge you to do this because I know you will benefit from it!

What have you got to lose?

_____

_____

_____

_____

What could you gain?

_____

_____

_____

_____

Personal Notes

5.4. Establish Your Plan

"Joe, I believe you're now ready to set some goals for yourself. First, I'd like to help you understand why goals are critical in your life. Imagine you and I are walking together into a dense pine forest. We come to a clearing about eighty to ninety yards across and walk to its center, and then you and I pick out a tree along the edge of the clearing. I give you a bow and arrow and tell you that your goal is to shoot the arrow into that tree trunk. But here's the catch: Before you shoot the arrow, I blindfold you and turn you around six or seven times so you don't know which direction you are facing. If I then have you load the arrow into the bow and shoot while blindfolded, how do you think you would do? There's a pretty slim chance of hitting the desired tree, right? That's what your life is like if you don't have clear, well-defined goals. Very simply, you can't hit what you want if you can't see it clearly.

"Joe, if you don't define where you want to go, you have very little chance of getting there. Then you end up wherever life takes you, which is probably some place you wouldn't choose. Sound familiar? I believe this is why you came to me for help. While you may have things you wish were true, you need a clear definition of what you want and a plan to help you achieve it. Otherwise you just have idle wishes, not goals.

"I hope you are beginning to see how goals are absolutely crucial. If you don't know clearly where you want to go and what you need to do to get there, it simply won't happen. Goals are really important, Joe! Do you get this?"

"I think I've got it!"

"Good! You have to understand three important aspects to a goal before it will motivate you into sustained action."

1. A goal has to elicit strong emotion. You must truly need it. Many people say they want to achieve goals. They even write them down but later give up on their goals because they want them but don't need them. Remind yourself daily why your goals are important to you!

2. A goal has to be realistic. In other words, if you truly have no way to make it happen but only wish it could be true, you will just frustrate yourself trying to achieve it. You should certainly stretch yourself beyond what you can achieve easily but not so far that you have no way of achieving it.

3. You have to define each goal in detail and set a specific point in time when you absolutely need to achieve it. There is no *someday* on your calendar; every goal you want to achieve must be tied to a specific date or it will probably float indefinitely and never be accomplished.

"So, Paul, with a clear, realistic definition and a defined completion date, a goal is really tied down. And I see where a strong emotional need is the driving force to make it happen."

"I'm glad you understand that all these factors (clear and realistic definition, specific date, and strong emotion) are critical to your future. Now that you understand the concept of a goal, let's talk about the various types of goals."

- Long-term goals are those you need to achieve within four to five years.
- Medium-term goals are those you need to achieve within one to three years.
- Short-term goals are those you need to achieve within the next twelve months to ensure that your medium-term and long-term goals can happen on schedule.

"Imagine a pyramid with the top section representing your long-term goals.

"The middle of the pyramid represents your medium-term goals and supports the top of the pyramid. The base of the pyramid represents your short-term goals, which support your medium-term goals.

As you achieve your short-term goals, or at least yearly, you need to evaluate your progress on all your goals, reevaluate your medium-term goals, and convert all possible ones to short-term goals. Similarly, make appropriate long-term goals into medium-term goals and restate your long-term goals.

"Joe, this concept applies to all your goals, personal or career. Please note: Aligning your goals with your priorities is critical to maintaining good personal balance!"

"That's a lot of structure, but it seems to provide checkpoints to help keep me on schedule."

"Yes, it does. Without this structure, your efforts to achieve goals will just float out of control, and the results will never be achieved. A description of the goal-setting process follows."

1. Define your long-term goals first. Be specific. Write them down and specify a target date four to five years in the future. You probably won't have a long list of these because they will be large, without as much detail as the goals that support them. Please note that you are to include goals within all your priority categories (for example, the Lord, other people, and yourself).

    For example, let's say you want to buy a home. This isn't going to happen without some planning and focused effort; therefore, it might fit within the four to five years of a long-term goal if you can create sufficient income. To make this goal specific, you need to research preferred locations and find out what a house in these locations might cost. Write down the locations and projected cost, including estimated closing costs. Take into account possible increases in value within the four-to-five-year period. Now you have a qualified long-term goal.

2. Define your medium-term goals. Be very specific and assign dates to each goal. Write them down. Most of these may support your long-term goals, but some may be independent of them. You will probably have more goals in this category, and details should be clearer than they are for your long-term goals. As you work toward these goals, some of the details may change a bit, so be sure to maintain an updated picture for each goal. Again, you need to include goals within all of your priority categories.

In your long-term goal of buying a home, you will estimate how much money you will need. You should plan on saving half of this amount within twenty-four to thirty months. Break this amount into monthly increments to save the needed amount within this time period.

You may also need to build up a good credit history to qualify for a home loan. Find out what is necessary to do this and take action as required to create the credit history.

If you have other medium-term goals, create a plan to make them happen too.

In each case, set dates for the achievement of your goals.

3. You should have many short-term goals. Define them and write them down in great detail. Again, some of these may be independent agendas, but most should support your longer-term goals. Assign dates to each goal within a twelve-month period. Include goals for all of your priority categories.

Monitor short-term goals on a weekly basis to stay on track. Have your chart in a place where you will see it daily to track your progress in real time.

To earn the money to save toward the home, for instance, you may have to get an additional job. If you are married, your spouse may need to work to provide additional savings. This must be accomplished very early in the first twelve months so you have time to accumulate the required money. If you let time slip by, you will need to save a greater amount per month to meet your longer-term goals. That's the reason to put this plan in place immediately.

If you are married and have no children, you may want to put off having children until your home is purchased. Children involve expenses you may not be able to afford while saving for a home.

Get a good investment advisor immediately so you can earn money on your savings right away. Good growth of your investments can be a valuable contribution to the home fund. Try to put off any unnecessary expenses during this time period, as money saved is truly the same as money earned when it comes to buying your home.

4. Put all your goals on a chart where you can easily read them every day to reinforce how important they are and keep on track to accomplish them.

5. Walk with a purpose and attack your goals with serious commitment to make them your reality. Do something every day to ensure achieving your goals on schedule.

Create positive affirmations to support your plan and repeat them to yourself multiple times each day. If you are truly committed to your goals, your purpose will be a force in your life. Keep the purpose alive with daily action and real-time accountability to your partner.

6. As you achieve individual goals, mark them off on your chart with a note of the dates when you completed them. That's what your chart is for. Use it!

7. Remember to review your goals frequently and upgrade them in real time as needed. For example, if you see that you are slipping behind in your schedule, you can double your efforts to make your goals happen as planned.

8. If you find you have set a goal to achieve something, but you are not doing what is required to achieve it as scheduled, reevaluate it. If it is no longer important to you, eliminate it.

A Note on Distractions

Expect to have interruptions—you will. Learn to identify these for what they are: either important matters that need your attention or distractions to avoid. By avoiding the unnecessary distractions, controlling your thoughts, and reviewing your goals at least every week, you can keep on course to achieve most of your goals on schedule.

"Can you do this, Joe?"

"I see that setting goals and making them happen requires a lot of focus."

"Yes, it does. But if your goals become your reality, would such focus be worth it?"

"Definitely. I've never had real purpose in my life, and I came to you because this is something I really want."

"Remember, Joe, just wanting a goal won't drive you to make it happen. You have to need it truly."

"I'm finally at the point where I really do need to change my life."

"I certainly hope so, because your future depends on it! And to make your goals happen, you will need to become accountable to somebody. We will discuss this in a future lesson. Today we are just discussing making goals. Joe, I want to caution you regarding three challenges in making goals."

• People almost always overestimate what they can achieve in a year. Similarly, people tend to underestimate what they can accomplish within four to five years. Be realistic in setting your goals because it is important to make these challenges achievable with determination and hard work.

• Be careful of deceiving yourself. It is quite common to say, 'I know what my goals are, so I don't have to review them regularly.' If you fall into this trap, you'd be wrong! Every step of this process is essential to making your life what you want it to be, so don't ever shortcut the process.

• Be sure your significant other supports you in what you want to achieve. This is especially true in areas related to finances, where a second income or delaying having children might need consideration as parts of your plan. No matter how committed you may feel to your goals, if your partner isn't on the same page with you, your goals, and possibly your relationship, will suffer. Looking at this issue from a different perspective, two people working together will have a stronger chance of attaining their common goals.

Stop. Think. Apply.

Make It Happen

Establish Your Plan

Highlights

- Without clear, realistic goals, you will certainly end up where you don't want to be!
- You may have to adjust your short-term goals to make them realistic. Be willing, though, to push yourself to achieve more than you have ever done in the past.
- Believe you can achieve your goals and embrace the discipline required to reach them.
- Positive self-talk and affirmations will help keep your belief strong.
- You can achieve anything you decide is important to you!

Application

Follow the goal-setting process discussed in the text and write down your goals—long-term, medium-term, and short-term goals. Be specific regarding your goals, required completion dates, and your driving emotion.

Note: Setting goals is crucial in finding your purpose and achieving greater personal fulfillment. You are responsible for your future! No one else will accept responsibility for it.

Long-Term Goals (4–5 years)	Due Date	Driving Emotion
_____	_____	_____
_____	_____	_____
_____	_____	_____
_____	_____	_____
_____	_____	_____
_____	_____	_____
_____	_____	_____

Medium-Term Goals (1–3 years)	Due Date	Driving Emotion
_____	_____	_____
_____	_____	_____
_____	_____	_____
_____	_____	_____
_____	_____	_____
_____	_____	_____
_____	_____	_____
_____	_____	_____
_____	_____	_____
_____	_____	_____
_____	_____	_____
_____	_____	_____
_____	_____	_____

Short–Term Goals (within one year)	Due Date	Driving Emotion
_____	_____	_____
_____	_____	_____
_____	_____	_____
_____	_____	_____
_____	_____	_____
_____	_____	_____
_____	_____	_____
_____	_____	_____
_____	_____	_____
_____	_____	_____
_____	_____	_____
_____	_____	_____
_____	_____	_____
_____	_____	_____

Important note: You must identify the emotional force driving you to achieve each goal. It is the reason that you will make each goal happen!

About Your Goals

What makes them so important to you?

_____
_____
_____
_____
_____
_____
_____

How do they support your priorities and purposes?

_____
_____
_____
_____

What do you fear if they don't happen?

_____
_____
_____
_____
_____
_____
_____
_____
_____
_____
_____
_____

Personal Notes

5.5. Attitude Is Everything!

"Joe, understand that setting goals is great, but unless you are totally committed to your action plan, it won't work. You need to keep your purpose alive and attack your plan with zeal. This is your life, so I hope you are ready to take ownership of your plan."

"I have to admit I'm somewhat intimidated by what we created."

"Whoa! 'We' didn't create your plan. I only guided you to understand what was required to create it. Are you trying to make me partly responsible for your plan?"

"No, I know you just guided me to create it."

"Are there things about this plan you don't like?"

"No, it's fine. I've just never done anything like this before."

"I understand your feelings, Joe, and it's natural to doubt yourself a bit, but as time goes on, you will get more comfortable. Positive affirmations can help you overcome doubt."

"Thank you for the reminder. I needed it."

"So, are you good with your plan?"

"Yes!"

"Then you need to implement your plan with conviction. You have thought long and hard about your cornerstones, and you have discovered (or rediscovered) an amazing purpose for a greater life. You have greatness within you that needs to be shared with the world!"

"I don't feel I have greatness yet, but I trust I can develop it by working my plan."

"I know you can! Now let's consider some attitudes essential to making your action plan successful.

"It's vital to be discerning and know when to say no. You need to be able to say *no* to propositions and input that don't help you toward your goals. Stay focused on activities that are uplifting rather than those that drain your energy. Use your energy in the most effective way. This could be applied to many venues. For example, say your friends want you to join a local club or sports team, but you are not really interested because you have a different focus (your goals). It is okay to decline. Or if you find yourself in the midst of tasks that are part of your plan but realize a given task will not create the end result you expected, quit that task! You don't want to become a serial quitter, but it is important to discern what is helpful and what is not and keep your focus on work that truly helps you accomplish your goals. Quitting an unproductive task is okay if you evaluate what you are doing and realize the task at hand detracts from your purpose."

"I often have trouble saying *no*, Paul," Joe noted, "because I don't want to disappoint anyone. How can I change my feelings on that?"

"If your purpose is strong enough, it will become natural to shed the distractions. Keep your goals in the front of your mind (that's why you read them regularly) and use your time wisely and purposefully. Do this each and every day, and you will be amazed at how you progress toward your goals. Perhaps something takes you away from your goals. The distraction could be any of many: spending too much time browsing social media, for instance, or always volunteering to do tasks for others. At any rate, you need to learn to say *no* for self-preservation. This is another element of maintaining balance. This isn't to say that you should never spend time on those activities, but you should limit and prioritize them. This gives you more time and freedom to pursue what really matters. Don't fill your life with activities that don't matter and might leave you no time for important ones. Joe, do you think you can put achieving your goals at a higher priority than pleasing other people?"

"Yes, I can, and I will! I've never had clearly defined goals before, and I'm excited about putting my plan into action. I've wanted a better life for a long time, and now I understand how to get it. I will make it happen!"

"I'm glad you are seeing the bigger picture, Joe! Another appropriate time to say *no* is to activities you find draining. You can outsource or delegate such activities. A client of mine, for example, found housework particularly draining. Not that many people actually love housework, but she hated it so much that it froze her into inaction. She never accomplished much when she was home because the housework was such a big emotional weight. I suggested that she outsource this task. This was a groundbreaking notion for her. She hired a young student to clean once a week. That $30 a week saved my client hours of agony. She was able to spend more time with her family, and lifting that heavy weight allowed her to be more effective in the other tasks she needed to accomplish.

"There are plenty of tasks you could potentially outsource, and you don't necessarily have to pay for it. You could trade time, for example, with someone who enjoys a particular task, and you could do a task that you enjoy for that person. Effective people, who have good balance in their lives, find the best ways to delegate. Outsourcing is a lot like delegating."

"I've never considered simply not doing something that I find draining."

"If you can say *no* to those tasks, Joe, say it. Use your brain power and energy more effectively!"

"How did you learn this, Paul?"

"Some trial and error over the years. The biggest boost for me was finding a valuable mentor! We'll talk about this later."

"Thank you! I won't forget this!"

"Good! I believe you *will* do well with this concept. Now onto the next key attitude.

"Mark Twain once said 'Eat a live frog first thing in the morning and nothing worse will happen to you the rest of the day.' [9] Sometimes you simply have to do something you won't enjoy—even as part of your action plan. Twain said to just do the task that you most dread, the task you hate, the task you feel is most draining first! By doing this you conserve your energy. It will be done and out of the way. The alternative is to procrastinate. Then the task will hang over your head and drag you down emotionally until you finally get to it. You don't have time or energy to put these tasks off. If you have to do it, just buckle down and get it done, leaving you free to move onto important things. If you can't decline a task, just get it out of the way. There will be tasks that you won't be able to avoid, but you can still keep your sanity by doing them first. Joe, is this a new concept for you?"

"Yes. I've never heard it before, but I can see where it makes sense. I've sometimes put off tasks I didn't want to do, but when I did finally get them done, I'd get past my guilt. I see that getting distasteful tasks out of the way first can take the load off me sooner."

"It's time to develop a new habit, Joe, and do what you dread most first. You will definitely like the freedom this gives you. You will be emotionally free to move onto the next task at hand instead of wasting your mental energy dreading the task you haven't done yet. Now onto the next key attitude: Keep proper focus. Be a laser, not a flashlight!

"Joe, consider the difference between shining a flashlight or a laser to focus on your goals on a pitch-black night. How far does a good flashlight project its light?"

"Not very far!"

"That's right. You can only see what is near you, which might be some of your short-term goals. A laser beam, however, shines very far, but only on a very specific target (like your primary, long-term goal). To stay motivated, you need to keep your eye on this long-term goal because it is the reward, the prize, the reason you created your goals and plan of action. It is imperative that this motivation involve a strong emotion like true need. If you have this level of commitment and stay focused on your goals, you won't be tempted by distractions outside your plan. Let me ask you, Joe, are you ready for this type of commitment?"

"It surely requires an intensity I've never had. Is this level of focus really required to achieve my goals?"

"Yes, it is. The key question is, 'How badly do you want to achieve your purpose in life and experience greater personal fulfillment?'"

"I really want it! You make me think back to why I came to you for help. Living my life like other people live theirs has left me feeling empty and unsatisfied. I need to have real purpose, and now you are telling me I need to have this laser focus on my goals or I won't achieve them. That's a huge change for my life."

"This type of focus is absolutely necessary if you really want a better life. If you truly want it, you will develop the attitudes that drive you to succeed. Are you getting it?"

"I've got it!"

"Good. Then let's move on and speak about how to take care of yourself and find a healthy balance! Do you feel balanced, Joe?"

"I'm not sure what you mean."

"While you need to focus your efforts on your goals like a laser beam, you also need an overall balance in your life to have a sense of inner peace. There are important aspects to being balanced: keeping your priorities straight, good allocation of your time, working effectively, getting sufficient rest, good nutrition, and regular exercise.

"And also, Joe, please remember that human nature can send us toward goals that seem attractive, such as accumulating money and power with a focus on self-importance. Becoming addicted to such a goal can destroy your balance, and following such a path toward success can cause you to lose what is truly important.

"Time is a limited resource, so it is essential to use your time each day effectively. Yes, you need to attack your goals fervently, but you also need to build breaks into your schedule to address your other priorities. You don't live in total isolation, and other people, principally your family, depend on you to help meet their needs too.

"The harder you work toward your goals, the more you need rest to maintain good balance.

Many studies have shown that taking breaks daily, weekly, and annually actually increases productivity. A big, fancy vacation is not required to give you the rest you need, but you have to give back to your mind and body to be effective.

"Joe, finding good balance is crucial for inner peace. While ensuring that you get sufficient rest, you also need to take care of your body with nutritious food and exercise. If you eat junk on the run most days, science, as well as anecdotal experience, shows that your brain will not function as well as it can."

"Sounds like I need to rearrange a few priorities to find better balance. I have not made taking care of myself a priority these last few years. And time with my family has suffered because I tend to respond to supposed emergencies at my job that probably could have waited until another day."

"It might seem difficult to create new habits, but I know you can do it! Once you create these habits, you will want to continue them. Remember, Joe, it only takes a month to establish a new habit. You can do just about anything for a month, right?"

"It's worth trying!"

"It's worth more than that. It's worth doing!"

Stop. Think. Apply.

Make It Happen

Attitude Is Everything!

Highlights

- Your goals and plans must be supported by determination and commitment.
- Stay focused and avoid distractions.
- Delegate tasks that are draining for you.
- Do your toughest task first each day.
- Keep your ultimate goal in sight. It will motivate you.
- Provide balance in your life, and you will be more productive.
- Take care of your mind and your body, and you will have more peace.

Application

Check yourself routinely. Distractions can seem worthy at the time, but be discerning and keep your focus where it needs to be.

Do certain things or people distract you regularly?
Make a list of them and count out those you can eliminate.

_____
_____
_____
_____
_____
_____

Are there particular tasks you hate doing and tend to put off? List them here.

_____
_____
_____
_____

Can you delegate or outsource any of those tasks?
Circle them in the previous list.
Now put a check by the tasks you need to do first each day.

How do you feel when you procrastinate?

_____

_____

_____

_____

Determine how you will stop procrastinating!
Yes, you really need to do this, so what are you going to do to make it happen?

_____

_____

_____

_____

What do you need to change to stay focused on your goals and maintain a balanced life too? Commit to doing everything in your power to make this happen!
Define what you need to do and are committed to doing.

_____

_____

_____

_____

Now define a daily routine that will balance your life while you work to achieve your goals, maintain your priorities, and satisfy your family and personal needs.
You probably won't do everything on your list every day, and that's okay. Just make sure you cover all the bases several times each week.
Yes, you can! Do it!

_____

_____

_____

_____

_____

_____

_____

_____

_____

_____

_____

_____

_____

- Find a quiet place where you can review how you are progressing toward your goals each week and determine if you are staying on target or missing goals you defined.
- Each week, write down your thoughts and feelings about your progress and date them. You need to get a journal for this purpose and keep it handy so you can do this on a regular basis. Weekly is best.

This regular review of your progress is vital to your journey and achieving your purpose, so don't skip it.

- If you need to adjust your goals, recommit yourself to your long-term goals and do whatever is necessary to make them happen by adjusting the time and effort you put into your shorter-term goals each week.
- Dream about how your life will be when you make your goals your reality and how you will feel about this achievement. Write these thoughts and feelings down in your journal too.

This is your life! So regularly reinforce your commitment to make it what you want it to be!

Personal Notes

5.6. Believe It. Do It. Live It!

"Joe, have you defined your goals in all three categories?"

"I have some goals written down, but I have some questions too."

"Good. You may have to take more time to finalize your goals. How can I help you?"

"You cautioned me about overloading my short-term goals and going too lightly on my long-term goals. How do I decide how long each task will take?"

"You may not get a realistic picture until you actually try to achieve your short-term goals. Remember, you need to make progress toward your goals on a consistent basis, so I encourage you to check your progress constantly. For example, at least once each week, make sure you can document significant progress. At the end of each month, determine if you have about 10–12 percent of the total work scheduled for that year completed. If you are not moving forward as you hoped, rededicate yourself to the task at hand and increase your efforts. Don't just revise your schedule. When six months have passed, you should see at least half of the project finished. Does this approach make sense, Joe?"

"Yes. But that's a lot more structure than I have ever had in my life."

"I understand how you feel. Until now, you have just coasted through life, without a defined plan and checkpoints to keep you on course. You now have a plan in place to make your ideal life happen. Do you really want your life to be the way you have envisioned it?"

"Yes. But as I look at what is required, I wonder if I can do it."

"If you look at how you have lived your life so far, that's a good question. However, if you look toward who you are becoming, you should have confidence that you can achieve anything you decide is important to you."

"You sound very sure of that."

"I am! And you need to see it with the same assurance I have. Setting goals for your future is good, but believing you really can accomplish those goals will make the difference between success and failure. I expect you to commit yourself to creating the reality you desire.

"Remember the story of the small locomotive that pulled a heavy load over the mountain. As he approached the mountain, he told himself, 'I think I can.' When he had succeeded, he told himself, 'I thought I could.' You have to talk to yourself the same way and really believe you can do it. Don't question or second-guess yourself."

"You make me feel I can do anything."

"You can, but you will need encouragement, guidance, and accountability along the way. This is where a mentor is important—to kick you in the butt if you slack off, take no excuses, and hold your feet to the fire to make you do what you need to do. Go over all your goals with this mentor and review your progress with him or her at least monthly. Twice a month is better. He or she will hold you accountable to actually accomplish your goals on time so you can live the ideal life you want. With this kind of support and your hard work, you will develop purpose in your life and create the personal fulfillment you desire."

"Is it normal to struggle with believing in myself?"

"Almost everyone does at some point. How can you help yourself strengthen your belief? Think back a few sessions."

"Oh! That's why constantly using positive self-talk and affirmations is important. I can see how I need to write down affirmations that support my purpose and my goals. This will help me believe in myself and guide me to fulfill my purpose. Thank you! This makes me feel more confident about actually achieving my goals. I never would have realized all you have taught me on my own."

"I enjoy teaching people how to find purpose and create ideal lives. Now it's up to you to make it happen. Expect me to check in with you periodically to see how you're doing."

Stop. Think. Apply.

Make it Happen

Believe It. Do It. Live It!

Highlights

- Make your short-term goals realistic but also stretch yourself to achieve big results.
- Embrace the discipline required to achieve your goals.
- Stay close to your mentor, who will hold your feet to the fire.
- Positive self-talk and affirmations will help keep your belief strong.
- You can achieve your purpose in life, and you will never regret doing so!

Application

- Once you start moving forward toward your goals, you should always be in the process of changing and growing into the person you are destined to be.
- Life isn't just about getting older. It's about continually becoming a better person!
- To make your life better, you have to do something most people won't do. Keep your ultimate goal in mind and focus on that day's goal even when you don't want to do it. Because if you just show up and put in the work every day, you will become all you are meant to be.
- If you drop out of this personal growth process, however, you will lose hugely. Somehow, someday, you will regret it!

Personal Notes

6. Summary and Final Encouragement

Summary

Your expectations and hopes for your life may not have been fulfilled by the reality you have experienced, and perhaps you currently seek guidance toward your purpose and greater personal fulfillment.

You should now understand the following points.

- Your personality, relationships, and experiences have made you who you are today.
- Your interests, talents, dreams, and passions define your individuality. They form a unique foundation on which to build your future.

Hopefully, you have discovered new possibilities to define your purpose and achieve greater personal fulfillment.

- We all have inner needs that can motivate us to act to satisfy them.
- Getting in touch with your inner needs is vital to achieving a significant purpose and personal fulfillment.
- Choosing a career and play-time activities that both support your inner needs is essential to fulfilling your purpose.
- Defining your top priorities provides guideposts to direct your decisions on a daily basis.

Recognize that what you do strongly affects the lives of people close to you. If you embark on a path that is contrary to your personal relationships, it can jeopardize those relationships. To make your life better, some factors have to change.

- Changing your life requires a decision to change; and only changing your thoughts and committed action with a well-designed plan can make it happen.
- Work your plan daily; check your progress weekly. Adjust your actions as required to ensure you are completing tasks on schedule.
- Be focused.
- Seek balance and take care of yourself.
- Be honest and open with your life partner and your mentor. Don't hold anything back. Good partners want your success as much as you do and will provide guidance and encouragement to help you achieve it.
- Believe in yourself. Be positive. Work your butt off. Expect to achieve your goals and fulfill your purpose.

Final Encouragement

- You are worthy of achieving your purpose and greater personal fulfillment!
- Never give in! Never give up!
- Keep learning and growing.
- Have hope! Every new day is a new beginning for the rest of your life.
- You are an amazing individual. Your dreams are worth fighting for!

Your life will be amazing when you fulfill your purpose on this earth.

Your enthusiasm for life will infect those around you. Go for it!

You are incredible! Just look at who you are and what makes you a unique individual! How will you change your life? How will you change the world?

Winston Churchill was one of the greatest statesmen of the twentieth century and served as prime minister of England during World War II. During this war, England was bombarded repeatedly by the Germans, and Churchill led his country with steadfastness and courage greater than most people believed possible.

Here are a couple of great quotes attributed to Churchill. [10]

- "The pessimist sees the problems in every opportunity. Whereas the optimist sees the opportunity in every problem."
- And, perhaps his most famous statement: "Never give in, never give in, never; never; never; never—nothing, great or small, large or petty—never give in except to conviction of honor and good sense."

I hope you remember his statements, which are both truthful and profound. Believe in yourself and never give in!

Expect life to give you challenges. It will. But by persevering through your challenges, you will develop endurance. And endurance develops strength of character, and character strengthens your confident hope. Hope will not lead to disappointment.

You have a unique purpose for living on this earth.

Seek it.

Find it.

Apply yourself to it.

Live it.

You will never regret doing this!

Afterword

I sincerely hope you have discovered a greater purpose for your life that leads you to a higher level of personal fulfillment.

I was chosen to produce this book, but I did not do it alone. I have been inspired and guided by God to make it happen. I firmly believe He wanted this book written and has used me to accomplish this result. Therefore, He deserves any honor and glory for how the book changes your life.

Sources

Official version of Meyers Briggs personality test is a paid test at www.meyersbriggs.org

Daniels, Ron, President of Daniels Wood Land, Inc., Paso Robles, CA, Statement made on his television series "Redwood Kings", 2017

Eggerichs, Dr. Emerson, *Love and Respect*, Nashville, TN, Thomas Nelson, 2008

Chapman, Gary, *The 5 Love Languages, Chicago, IL*, Northfield Pub., 2015

Sayers, Gale, *I Am Third*, 1st Ed. The Viking Press, 1970, 2nd Ed. Harmondsworth, Middlesex, UK, Penguin Books, 2001

Aitchison, Steven: One of his many quotes on the Internet

Tracy, Brian, *Eat That Frog*, Berrett Koehler Publishers, Inc., San Francisco, CA, 2nd Edition, 2007

Churchill, Winston, "Never Give In", Harrow School, London, UK, October 29, 1941, Speech

About the Author

Robert's career includes aerospace engineering and design/manufacturing process improvement for large, high-tech and manufacturing companies.

Throughout his life people have sought his counsel regarding finding purpose and fulfillment in their lives, and he has guided many of them to greater levels of personal success. He was led to produce this book to reach a larger audience.

Printed in the United States
By Bookmasters